Managing Your Life and Time

Managing Your Life and Time

Jo Berry

PYRANEE
BOOKS

Zondervan Publishing House
Grand Rapids, Michigan

MANAGING YOUR LIFE AND TIME
Copyright © 1986 by Jo Berry

Pyranee Books are an imprint of Zondervan Publishing House, 1415 Lake Drive, S.E., Grand Rapids, Michigan 49506

Library of Congress Cataloging in Publication Data

Berry, Jo.
  Managing your life and time.

  "Pyranee books."
  Bibliography: p.
  1. Christian life—1960–   . 2. Time management—Religious aspects—Christianity. I. Title.
BV4501.2.B4168   1986   248.4   86-11049
ISBN 0-310-34181-7

Edited by Kathy Heetderks
Designed by Ann Cherryman

Unless otherwise noted, all Scripture references are taken from the New American Standard Bible.

Printed in the United States of America

86 87 88 89 90 91 / 10 9 8 7 6 5 4 3 2 1

CONTENTS

To Fritz Ridenour, in gratitude for his expertise, his commitment to excellence, his faith in me, and his unrelenting blue pencil, which always teach, inspire, and encourage

Introduction

One of the questions I'm most frequently asked when I conduct seminars and teach Bible studies is "How can I find the time to do everything I want and need to do?" That question, which obviously reflects a need, prompted me to write this book. At first, I intended to write about time management, but as I prayed, thought about, and outlined the contents, I realized time-management problems are a symptom of an undisciplined lifestyle.

You can't manage your time unless and until you discipline your mind, spirit, will, and body. Consequently, this book is about self-management, as well as time management. It may raise as many questions as answers when you take a deep, introspective look at the way you live; it certainly should make you think. I hope you will be motivated and challenged to take charge of your life and make the most of every moment.

Managing Your Life and Time is a book you do, as well as read. It is based on scriptural principles and can be used for individual or group studies. The workshops at the end of each chapter are designed to help you, the reader, internalize the contents, take inventory, and learn how to manage your time and your life.

Remember, it's your life and how you live it is up to you!

Chapter One   CHOOSE LIFE!

"See, I have set before you today life and prosperity, and death and adversity . . . so choose life" (Deuteronomy 30:15, 19).

I couldn't help overhearing two women who were sitting directly behind me on the bleachers at the Little League field. One was complaining that her life was a rat race. "I never have any time to myself," she claimed. "My house is always a mess; the kids and Bill never help. No matter what I do it's never enough, and no one notices anyway. Sometimes I feel like running away from home," she joked.

Her friend laughed. "I know what you mean. I just keep telling myself that as bad as life is, it beats the alternative."

Sadly, their comments and their situations are all too common. Many people feel frustrated, frantic, unappreciated, and used. Life is something that happens *to* them: They're caught up in it but seem to have little control over it. Actually, people who let life happen to them instead of seizing and savoring it aren't living at all; they're merely existing. There is a marked difference between the two perspectives.

Edward Young noted, "Time *wasted* is existence; *used* is life."[1] Existing means continuing to be; living means abounding with force and energy. Existing is passive; living is active. People who exist let things happen *to* them; people who choose life make things happen *for* them. People who exist stagnate in their circumstances; people who live grow beyond or alter theirs.

Last summer, George, Brian, and I went to Jackson, Wyoming, and took a four-hour, white-water raft trip. Our only participation was to admire the scenery and, at critical times, hold lifelines and squeal as we were bobbled and drenched. If it hadn't been for our guide, a one-hundred-pound wisp of a girl who manipulated that huge raft as deftly as I handle my station wagon with power steering, we'd have been swept along with the current, likely landing on the rocks. As passengers, we were like people who exist; we were completely passive except for following our guide's instructions. She, on the other hand, exemplified life: She took charge of the situation. She steered the craft, carefully studied the movement of the water, watched for danger, plotted a course, and combated those rapids. She didn't make them go away or change them; rather, she conquered them. That's what living is about.

In "Psalm of Life," Henry Wadsworth Longfellow wrote, "Life is real! Life is earnest! And the grave is not its goal." We don't live to die but to *matter*—to be productive, to be useful, and to have made some difference that we've lived at all. The Lord's challenge to His people through the prophet Moses is "choose life!" Stop existing. Opt for prosperity over adversity. Surely each of us would rather prosper—thrive, flourish, and bear fruit—than be mired in adversity. However for myriads of reasons, many of us don't know how to choose life. If we are going to become active participants in our fate rather than passive observers of it, we need to learn how to manage our time and lives.

IT'S UP TO YOU

Life management embodies eight major components. The first is *CHOICE*. Many people act from habit: They do what they do, go where they go, shop where they shop, believe what they believe because it's what they've always done. They do not think in terms of alternatives: They do not realize they can alter their circumstances by choosing how they respond to them rather than assuming they are trapped in them.

In a Bible study I attend, we recently discussed how women approach their work, both in the home and in the marketplace. One woman shared that for most of her life she had worked at what other people had told her she should do. She had always hated and resented what she'd done. "Then," she said, "for the first time in my life, three years ago, I picked my job strictly because it was something *I* wanted to do. There are still times when I don't like working, but all in all, I love what I do not so much because of what it is but because it was my choice. So, I can live with the consequences."

That woman learned two valuable lessons: There's something about choosing that produces dignity and makes us feel good about ourselves; and we *can choose* how we will approach life and assimilate time. "You don't get to choose how you're going to die. Or when. You can only decide how you're going to live."[2]

How encouraging to know that you don't have to stay locked into situations that debilitate you or maintain static, meaningless relationships. You can change your mind, search out new ideas, expand your horizons, and seek solutions to your problems. It's your life. How you live it is up to you.

Sometimes, we are afraid to start managing our lives because we fear we'll make mistakes. That's right. Each of us will, but there's nothing wrong with making an honest error in judgment. Making a wrong or inappropriate choice isn't a sin or a sign of failure or weakness; it's an indication that we're human. Richard J. Needham noted, "Strong people make as many and as ghastly mistakes as weak people. The difference is that strong people admit them, laugh at them, learn from them. That is how they became strong."[3] Choosing strengthens our minds and our character.

At other times, people let others make their choices for them because they don't want to accept the responsibility that choosing brings. They know that if they start exercising their God-given gift of choice, they'll have only themselves to blame if things don't go well. They're right. But God holds each person accountable for every choice he makes, including the choice to abdicate the responsibility to choose. God's instruction is clear: *Choose life!* Employing the freedom of choice is part of life management.

MAKING CHANGES

Making choices forces us to make changes. *Change* is the second component of life management. The poet Goethe observed, "Life belongs to the living and he who lives must be prepared for changes." Choosing life means we will grow and change. Babies mature into adults; planted seeds ripen into fruit-producing plants; new concepts and thoughts grow into actions and attitudes. Change is uncomfortable for many of us. Stepping out on untried ground is frightening. As boring as it is, the status quo is more comfortable than the insecurities that lurk in the shadows of the unknown.

THE FEAR OF CHANGE

Life management involves what the Bible calls "reproof," which means that we sift through our beliefs and behavior to prove to ourselves whether they are valid and then change the ones that aren't. Many of us are reluctant to do that. It's easier to judge others than ourselves, to ask how they can possibly believe as they do instead of examining ourselves. Why? Because deep in our souls we know if we ask, "Why do I believe as I do?" we may have to change.

Why do we fear change? Why does it make us so uncomfortable? Perhaps it's because we've been conditioned to accept and assimilate information that is fed to us rather than to think and formulate opinions for ourselves. We accept as true whatever is programed into our minds through radio, television, and audio and video tapes. Examining all sides of every issue and being open to new ideas and various schools of thought isn't as easy as sticking with the status quo or letting others do our thinking for us. Yet, change can be a constructive force for good and growth in our lives.

Psychologists have discovered that introducing new ideas into our lives and doing things differently form new pathways in the brain. As a result, changing the way we think and act opens channels that help us develop the ability to adapt and find new ways to solve problems: It helps us think creatively.

Perhaps we're afraid of change because we don't like to deal with the negative reactions of others who are affected by the changes. I know a woman who is a recovering alcoholic. Her greatest disappointment was that her family reacted so negatively when she stopped drinking. She had thought they would be overjoyed, but they were upset by the changes her sobriety made in their lives.

Another reason we are discomforted by change is because change involves breaking bonds: We are forced to leave one thing and go on to another. A study done at the Menninger Clinic in Topeka, Kansas, in the late seventies showed that when we change, for the better or worse, voluntarily or involuntarily, we experience loss because we have to give up the old and familiar to move on to the new and untried.

I happen to be a person who enjoys change. I love trying new things, meeting new people, and stepping into the unknown, but I also suffer loss when changes occur. In 1969, when we adopted our son Brian, I decided to quit teaching and devote myself to being a homemaker and establishing a writing career. Those were both things I wanted to do. So in June of that year, I resigned my position as a reading specialist with the Los Angeles City Schools, terminating a rewarding, challenging ten-year career. I lost a lot when I made that shift: the pleasure of working with children and helping to mold their minds, a set salary and an upwardly mobile, successful career, the stimulating intellectual and social contact with my colleagues, and a certain amount of status.

When school opened that September, I wondered what was happening and missed being there. Although we were in the process of buying a new home and I had an adorable new baby, I felt incomplete, like a part of me was missing. Even now, fifteen years later, I'm struck by a sense of loss when I drive by an elementary school. Change *is* uncomfortable because it involves loss, so we resist it.

I believe the main reason we avoid change is because we've been conditioned to believe change is bad. We don't like change because it disrupts the ongoing scheme of things, that cocoon of complacency called the status quo. So when we change, whether it's an attitude, an opinion, or our behavior, someone invariably points an accusing finger at us and says, "You shouldn't be doing that because it's different." What they really mean is that we're making them uncomfortable. Actually, uniformity and conformity stifle progress. Someone once said that the opposite of courage isn't cowardice; it's conformity. We can't learn to manage our lives and time unless we are willing to risk changing.

TAKING CHARGE OF YOUR LIFE

A third important aspect of life management is *control.* You cannot manage your life until you take charge of it, accept responsibility for the choices you make, and deal with the results. Think for a moment. Are you controlling your life? Does it seem you're always caught in the middle because so many people are making demands of you? Does it seem that you're involved in so many things you're a slave to your calendar? Do you consistently seek counsel before making decisions and usually go with the *majority* opinion? Do you unthinkingly let others impose their wills on you? If you have responded yes to these questions, you're relinquishing control of your life to others. The more control you release, the more frustrated and resentful you become, and the resulting helplessness creates an enormous amount of stress.

Recently a young woman phoned me from the East Coast. She said she had read several of my books and studied some of my tapes. She wondered if she would be imposing if she asked me for an objective opinion about a problem she was having: "I'm twenty-seven years old, single, and have a degree in marketing. I've been offered a lucrative promotion within my firm but accepting it means moving to the Midwest. My dad doesn't think I should go because I've never been away from my family, except when I went to college, which was only ninety miles from home. Mom doesn't think I should go either. She says I'd hate living in a large city and it isn't a safe place for a single girl. My brother and his wife say my parents are being overly protective and I should go because it would be good for me. My two best friends think I should accept the promotion but don't want me to leave."

"Stop!" I interrupted when she paused to take a breath. "Let me ask you a question. What do *you* want to do?"

After a long pause, she laughed, "You know, I haven't thought much about that."

We talked for several minutes. I told her I couldn't advise her what to do about the job. Instead, I suggested she forget all of the conflicting counsel she'd received, stop collecting opinions, and think for herself. I told her she might benefit from getting away alone for a weekend to think and pray through the situation. I suggested she compile a list of pros and cons and then make a decision based solely on what was best for her and what she wanted to do.

A few months later, I received a letter postmarked Kansas City. She wrote she had never realized how out of control her life had been and how frightening and exciting taking charge of it could be.

No one has the right to tell anyone else how to live in adult relationships, but practically everyone will if we let them. Letting other people, a group, or an organization tell us how we should live, how we should spend our time, or what we should believe is like driving down the highway at high speed without holding onto the steering wheel. We have no control over where we are going, and that can be deadly.

In some ways, it's easier to respond and react than to assert ourselves. Passivity is safer. If things turn out wrong, we can always blame the people who imposed their will on us by claiming we were only doing what was expected. As an example, if my young friend had turned down that promotion and later realized she had made a mistake, she could have sidestepped responsibility by blaming all who advised her to stay. We should not rely on others to interpret God's will for us, no matter how well intentioned or close to us they are. Scripture teaches that each of us is accountable to work out his *own* salvation. We're abdicating that God-assigned responsibility if we refuse to take control of our lives.

Control isn't demanding your own way. Nor is it a license for self-indulgence—doing what one pleases, when one pleases, without consideration for anyone else's feelings. There is a certain amount of restriction in any situation.

Control isn't trying to make others conform to our standards or fit into our plans by imposing ourselves or our beliefs on them but living according to positive principles we have determined are best for us. Control is performing to the utmost of our abilities within the boundaries of God's sovereign will and taking command of every circumstance.

MAINTAINING CONTROL

Claiming control of our lives is only the first step in the ongoing, moment-by-moment process of life management. J. H. Chitwood observed, "Life is a continuous experience but God gives it to us in stages—one day at a time." After we initially take charge, we have to maintain control. I call this fourth component of life management *administrating*. Administrating includes three phases: *analyzing, organizing* and *supervising*.

Analyzing means to assess opportunities and to determine which ones we should pursue. We must carefully weigh the pros and cons in every situation, decide what our options are, and which of them to exercise. During the span of our lives, most of us will come to many crossroads where we have to decide which route to take. Some are simple: We can go straight ahead or stop where we are. Others, such as which career to choose, when or if to marry and have children, or whether to accept a promotion that means a transfer across the country, are like major intersections. There are many possible directions to turn and many signals to decipher. Analyzing helps us make wise decisions, categorize information, and consider alternatives in an orderly, thoughtful way.

Administrating also includes *organizing*—doing whatever is necessary to keep peace and order in our lives while simultaneously accomplishing everything we want and need to do. We organize by setting goals and establishing priorities. Goals define what we want to accomplish. They are tangibles we can work for, such as a different job or a new house. Priorities are activities that help us reach goals.

For example, if your goal is to change jobs, you may need to set aside time to update your education and skills, so you'll be properly trained when you apply. You'll definitely need to prepare a resume and read the Help Wanted columns or contact an employment agency. Then, you'll have to prioritize those activities—decide what you need to do and when and how to do it—to accomplish your goal.

To establish goals you have to decide what you want to do with your life now, a month from now, a year from now, and in the distant future. Your goals determine what your lifestyle will be. Because they are part of life, they will change and vary.

When I was growing up (are you ready for this?), I wanted to be a private detective. When I first started seriously writing, I was convinced I didn't want to write books, just short stories, articles, and curriculum. Obviously, my thinking has changed since this is my eleventh book, but my long-range goal to become a published author hasn't.

Priorities are more fickle than goals, so they need to be established daily and sometimes shifted or revised throughout the day. We'll talk later more about how to do that.

Finally, administrating our lives means *supervising*. Once you take charge of your life, you become your own supervisor. You are primarily accountable to yourself and to the Lord for what you do. Every so often—not too infrequently—you need to sit back and take an insightful, objective look at what you're doing, how well you're doing it, and why you're doing it. Every time you encounter a problem, you need to determine if anything you did contributed to it and if you could have done something to prevent it. Productive administrating means constantly monitoring how efficiently and effectively you're managing your life and time.

ROLL WITH THE PUNCHES

As we gain and maintain control over our lives, set goals, establish priorities, and evaluate performance, we naturally develop a plan, that is, we set up schedules and inaugurate routines. That's good. But as with any good thing, we need to be careful not to overdo. We can become so organized that our agenda controls us instead of the other way around. *Flexibility* is the fifth relevant component in life management. The reason we prioritize and organize our activities is to help us distribute our time, so we can do everything we want and need to do. Scheduling should relieve, not create, stress. Sometimes people are so tied to self-imposed time-tables they cannot relax and enjoy life.

Ralph Waldo Emerson observed, "Life is a series of surprises." How true! We don't know what's going to happen from one minute to the next. We mustn't become so intractable that we forget how to roll with the punches.

Schedules should provide a framework for what we do. They should move us forward, not box us in. They *do not* have to be followed to the letter every single moment of every single day. Part of successful life management is being flexible enough to allow for the unexpected, to restructure priorities and shift plans without feeling guilty or getting upset. Columnist Sidney J. Harris wisely wrote, "The art of living successfully consists of being able to hold two opposite ideas in tension at the same time: first, to make long-term plans as if we were going to live forever; and second, to conduct ourselves daily as if we were going to die tomorrow."[4] As Christians, we should be able to sense the moving of the Spirit in our lives instead of categorizing His activity as a disruption in our routine.

LET'S HAVE FUN

Someone once said, "Humor oils the wheels of life and helps to keep it running smoothly." It won't matter much how wisely you make choices, how many positive changes you initiate, how adeptly you control and administrate your life and time, or how flexible you are if you can't have fun in the process. *Enjoyment* is the sixth vital ingredient in life management.

Sometimes we take life and God far too seriously. The

Westminster Confession of Faith declares it is our Christian duty to *enjoy* God. Laughter is as instinctive as tears. When something funny happens, our natural, normal human response is to chuckle or giggle. The Preacher who penned Ecclesiastes affirmed there *is* a time to laugh.

I used to puzzle over why the Holy Spirit didn't direct the authors of the Gospels to write, "Jesus laughed," as well as "Jesus wept." I've decided the reason is because it's so obvious that the Lord would laugh, it goes without saying. Each of us laughs many times every day, certainly more often than we cry. Jesus was human, as well as divine, so of course He laughed. He enjoyed life, relished close friendships, and took great pleasure in being with children.

Jesus wants us to enjoy life! He promised us full joy when we abide in Him. Enjoying what we do and savoring the pleasures Christ sets before us are by-products of the prosperity we experience when we choose life.

KNOW YOURSELF

A seventh component of life management is *self-knowledge*. You are a composite of everything that has happened to you up to this moment. Multitudes of people and events have touched your life. You have formulated opinions about yourself based on selected data you have invented or received from others and have accepted as valid—*whether it is or not.* Error, as well as truth, has been programed into your thinking. You need to acquire a balanced, accurate perspective about yourself before you can adequately manage your life. As J. B. Phillips paraphrased, "try to have a sane estimate of your capabilities" (Rom. 12:3 PHILLIPS).

We all nurture misconceptions about ourselves that eventually become self-fulfilling prophecies. For example, Amy believed she wasn't good at math, so she never learned to balance her checkbook. Sarah was convinced she was clumsy, so she wouldn't sign up for a much-needed fitness class. Diane thought she didn't have any mechanical ability, so she never learned how to change a washer in the sink or check oil in her car. Like these women, we defeat ourselves with lies about who we are or what we're capable of doing.

Anyone who can use a calculator and read the simple, easy-to-follow instructions on the back of a bank statement can learn to balance a checkbook. Exercise improves coordination, which is a reason, not an excuse, to participate in a fitness program. Doing simple, mechanical chores doesn't require mechanical aptitude but the ability to follow directions. Self-knowledge starts with shifting our mental attitude into neutral, objectively evaluating ourselves, and deprograming misconceptions.

Because we've been conditioned to believe that self-love and self-acceptance are egotistical, most of us have difficulty appraising ourselves. However, we cannot be happy and whole until we develop an honest, balanced understanding of who we are. We cannot take charge of our lives until we identify both our strengths and weaknesses, positive qualities and faults. Once we get to know ourselves, we will be better equipped to manage our time and our lives.

GETTING TO KNOW GOD

The final and most important aspect of life management is *getting to know God*. He is the One who created us, so He understands us better than we will ever understand ourselves. He knows our physical and emotional strengths and limitations. He alone has a complete, comprehensive knowledge of what each of us is like.

If I want something done, I go to someone who is qualified. When my car needs to be repaired, I take it to an auto mechanic. When my hair needs to be cut, I go to a hairdresser who specializes in naturally curly hair. When I took writing courses, I enrolled in the best school I could find.

If you want to learn how to manage your life and your time, consult the Expert who gave them to you. Who is better qualified to show you how to choose, change, control, administrate, and enjoy life? Who can reveal yourself to you? The Lord who gives life can show us how to choose life.

WORKSHOP

1. Read Deuteronomy 30:11–20. On the chart below list what the passage says you must do to choose life. Then list God's promises to those who do.

Your Responsibility	God's Promise

2. What results of disobedience—choosing death and adversity—are listed in the passage?

3. The following statements will help you analyze how well you manage your life and your time. Write the appropriate response in the blank: never, seldom, sometimes, usually, always.
   a. I *live* rather than merely exist. _____
   b. I exercise my God-given freedom of choice. _____
   c. I maintain control of my life. _____
   d. I resist change. _____
   e. I accept responsibility for the choices I make. _____

f. I let other people impose their will on me. _____

g. I analyze the pros and cons in every situation. _____

h. I set goals and work toward them. _____

i. I establish priorities daily. _____

j. I evaluate my behavior and performance. _____

k. I am flexible and roll with the punches. _____

l. I enjoy most of what I do. _____

m. I enjoy the relationships in which I'm involved. _____

n. I know myself well. _____

o. I cling to self-defeating "I'ms." _____

p. I am consistently affected by the past. _____

q. I know God well. _____

r. I consistently work at knowing God better. _____

4. Study your answers. For each negative response you gave in question three, write one specific thing you can do to start overcoming the problem.

Chapter Two

THE GOD FACTOR

"If thou wilt . . . thou shalt find the knowledge of God"
(Proverbs 2:1, 5 KJV).

It's one thing to decide you want to manage your life and your time better; it's another thing to do it. How do you determine what to do and how to do it? Where do you begin?

None of us can change his entire lifestyle in a moment. Yet, that's usually what we try to do. That's why New Year's resolutions generally aren't effective. We decide that at a given moment, 12:01 A.M. on January 1, we will make dozens of drastic alterations in our lives. We vow to stop smoking, lose fifteen pounds, quit eating desserts, exercise every day, stop procrastinating, get up fifteen minutes earlier every morning to have devotions, and promise the Lord and ourselves we'll read through the Bible in a year.

If you truly want to change, you need to establish a definite starting point. Then, focus on transforming one specific area before undertaking another. Regardless of how sincere you are or how noble your intentions, when you try to restructure your life in one grandiose gesture, you've programed yourself for failure. Trying to modify everything at once is impossible and unwieldy. Josh Billings aptly said, "It is easy to assume a habit; but when you try to cast it off, it will take skin and all." Restyling habits takes concentration and effort. Sometimes it's painful, like pulling a Band-Aid from a wound that's healing.

Your natural inclination will be to start managing your life by manipulating externals, such as shifting schedules and reorganizing or eliminating activities. But you cannot permanently restructure your performance by rearranging your activities any more than you can restructure the floor plan of a house by rearranging the furniture. Instead, you need to begin by getting to know God. Then, with His help, you can revamp the internal.

CULTIVATE A RELATIONSHIP

Although I listed *Getting to Know God* as last of the eight major components in life management, it is the first and most crucial step. He can help us define our capabilities and limitations by revealing our shortcomings to us, show us how to grow by helping us change, and how to properly manage our lives and our time. Getting to know God sounds like quite an undertaking, but it isn't as complicated as we might think. We can start by doing what we do when we want to get to know anyone: We can cultivate a relationship with Him.

J. I. Packer, author of *Knowing God,* noted, "To get to know another person you have to commit yourself to his company and interests, and be ready to identify yourself with his concerns."[1] We get to know God as we commit ourselves to His company: spend time with Him, share our thoughts, hopes, dreams, failures, and frustrations with Him, talk with and listen to Him, identify with His interests and concerns, and work at building a relationship with Him. Sometimes we forget the Father and Christ and the Holy Spirit are *persons.* We envision God sitting on His throne in heaven, confine Jesus to history, and limit the Spirit to the pages of Scripture. In actuality, each is a person who can be an ever-present, positive influence in our lives.

Sometimes intimate, ongoing relationships suffer because they are taken for granted. A husband forgets to tell his wife he loves her. Parents of good students expect all A's and B's on their children's report cards but forget to praise them for their efforts. We expect our friends to do us favors and tolerate our thoughtlessness.

Sometimes, we take our relationship with God for granted in much the same way. We know He is always there, but we forget to tell Him we love Him or to express appreciation. We presume on His grace and automatically expect His blessings. We unintentionally exclude Him from the moment-by-moment business of living by neglecting to seek Him more than by consciously turning away. We must remember that relationships don't happen instantaneously; rather, they grow and are refined through constant, detailed attention. We get to know the Lord better as we become more aware of Him *as a person* and thoughtfully cultivate our relationship with Him.

LEARNING WHO GOD IS

Search the Scriptures

Another way to get to know God is by exploring His Word. People who meet me frequently tell me they feel like they already know me because they've listened to my tapes or read my books. In much the same way, every page of Scripture reveals something to us about God: how He thinks and feels, acts and reacts, speaks and keeps silence. The Word is somewhat like a sacred diary in which the Almighty exposes Himself to us in intimate, understandable detail. Through His encounters with the saints of old, we learn how God approaches and responds to His people. Then, we understand a little better how God will approach us when we see how He spoke to the woman at the well or how He rebuked David. The Bible reveals God's magnificence and glory in terms we can understand because its pages are filled with vivid sketches that reveal His nature and personality.

I took a writing course several years ago. The first

assignment was to write three paragraphs describing my character and personality. That assignment was easy because I didn't have to do any research or verify facts. Everything I wrote was accurate and also revealing, since I could tell things about myself that no one else knew. At the bottom of the assignment sheet the professor had written, *"When I read this, I should feel like I know You!"*

In Scripture, through His chosen servants, the Holy Spirit penned thousands of paragraphs describing God's character and personality. Every word is accurate and extremely revealing because the Lord wrote the material. The Bible is His autobiography. As we read and study it, we should start to feel as if we know Him.

Look at Jesus

But sometimes, deciphering the inspired words into living reality is hard because relating to a Spirit or an unseen God is difficult. To overcome that identification problem, God graciously gave us an object lesson—someone concrete for us to relate to—He sent His son. If we want to know what God is like, we can look at Jesus. John wrote, "No man has seen God at any time; the only begotten God, who is in the bosom of the Father, He has explained Him" (John 1:18). Paul noted that Jesus "is the [visible] image of the invisible God" (Col. 1:15), a photographic replica of the Father.

The Son shows us what the Father is like. God's love is seen in the way Jesus ministered to children, commended the widow who gave everything she had, patiently trained His disciples, and forsook His authority to take on human form. The Father's omniscience is mirrored in the way Christ read the mind of His accusers and answered them *before* they asked their questions. His compassion is reflected in the tears He shed when Lazarus died and in the gentle way He responded to the untouchables of society and healed the sick. His faithfulness is manifested in each step He took on the painful road to Calvary. Looking at Jesus helps us to know God better, so does looking at ourselves.

Look at Ourselves

Because all human beings are created in the image of God, we can learn something about what He is like by comparing ourselves to Him. We all have emotions and express them. We all have intellects: We can think, reason, and draw conclusions. We all need love, companionship, acceptance, and understanding. These human characteristics are reflective of our "godlikeness."

God has and expresses emotions. Moses spoke about the Lord rejoicing (Deut. 30:9). Isaiah declared that the Lord would suffer anguish of soul (Isa. 53:11). Numerous times in Scripture God's anger is kindled by man's unrighteousness. The psalmists repeatedly exalt His compassion: Psalm 136 alone mentions God's lovingkindness twenty-six times.

God also thinks, understands, and reasons. During the time of the prophet Isaiah, the Lord urged His people to come and reason with Him (Isa. 1:18). David seemed overwhelmed by the immensity of God's intellect that also focuses on individuals. He wrote, "Many, O Lord my God, are the wonders which Thou hast done, and Thy thoughts toward us . . . if I would declare and speak of them, they would be too numerous to count" (Ps. 40:5).

The Lord revealed something about Himself by creating us in His image. Examining our godlikeness can help us get to know God.

Look at Others

Godly role models are another resource for exploring the attributes of God. We can learn a great deal about Him by watching other Christians who are walking in the Spirit and honoring His Word. Paul boldly charged the Corinthians to "be imitators of me, just as I also am of Christ" (1 Cor. 11:1).

Although my mother died when I was thirteen, I have learned many things about what a godly woman should be and what God is like by reflecting on her example. She was totally devoted to her husband and children. Nothing we said or did could alter her love or loyalty toward us. God is devoted to His children in exactly that way.

My mother was a merciful woman who was always willing to forgive or give someone the benefit of a doubt, just as God is gracious and forgiving.

She was faithful, like God's faithfulness. Every morning she spent a few minutes reading her Bible and a devotional booklet. Every night before she went to bed she prayed and read the Bible again. Every Saturday night she studied her Sunday school lesson, so she would be prepared and could contribute in class.

She was reverent and obedient, just like Jesus showed us to be. As a deaconess in our church, one of her duties was to prepare Communion. I looked forward to helping her and the other women pour the grape juice into the little glasses and break the unleavened bread into pieces and arrange them neatly on the shiny silver trays. I remember that Mom never let me snitch a drink or a bite because, she explained, that particular juice and matzo had been set aside as sacred, representing Jesus' body and blood. She said that being Communion elements made what was common special. Communion has always been more precious to me because of her respect for the service and symbolism of the elements.

Each of us learn about God from watching other Christians who emulate Him, as I learned about Jesus by watching my mother so many years ago.

GOD IN LIFE MANAGEMENT

Halloween just passed. Here in Los Angeles, several of the local television stations had "horror marathons," showing horror movies all afternoon and evening on October 31. When I was reading through the program guide, I was fascinated with the descriptions of the movies. One was advertised as "the chilling tale of an innocent girl who becomes possessed by the evil spirit of her dead sister, who died under mysterious circumstances while practicing witchcraft, and terrorizes an entire town with her ghostly antics." Another was about a demon-haunted house and its efforts to possess and control the family who had just moved in.

Usually, we associate being possessed by a spirit with the occult and the powers of darkness. We forget that Christians are also possessed by the Holy Spirit. Once we commit our lives to Christ, the Holy Spirit dwells within us and aims to control us. J. H. Jowett said, "I shall be God possessed. He will dwell in me. And where He dwells, He controls. If He lives in my life He will direct my powers. It will not be I that speak, but My Father that speaketh in me. He will govern my speech. He will empower my will. He will enlighten my mind. He will energize and vitalize my entire life." That is how the God Factor works in life management.

Let's examine how the Lord supplies the spiritual depth and dimension that are necessary for us to manage our lives and time in a manner that is pleasing to Him, brings fulfillment to us, and blesses others.

CONSIDERATE CHOICES

We have established that each of us must choose how to live. For Christians, that right to choose doesn't mean we may be uncaring or inconsiderate. Our God-given gift of choice must be tempered by careful application of Christian responsibility. Willingness to adjust to others as we make choices is evidence of God's presence in our lives.

There are three God Factors to consider as each of us makes choices: motive, method, and results. Why am I making this choice? *How* can I implement it in a godly way? *What* will be the results?

Motives Matter

Jesus taught both with His actions and His words that every choice we make should be motivated by love. We are, after all, possessed by the God of love. When asked which commandment in the Law was greatest, He replied, *"You shall love the Lord your God with all your heart, and with all your soul, and with all your mind. This is the great and foremost commandment. The second is like it, you shall love your neighbor as yourself. On these two commandments depend the whole Law and the Prophets"* (Matt. 22:37–40). In other words, Christ believed that love is the essence of the Law. It's what makes it work, what makes it real, what makes it matter.

In Christian ethics, doing things lovingly is more important than doing them correctly. Jesus was always concerned with motives. After He told His disciples that He had to go to Jerusalem and suffer many things and be killed, Peter, who loved the Lord dearly, was devastated. He took Jesus aside and tried to dissuade Him: "God forbid it, Lord! This shall never happen to you" (Matt. 16:22).

Peter's reaction appeared quite normal for the circumstances: He cared; he was concerned; he didn't want his dear friend to suffer, much less die. His motives seemed pure, but they weren't. Jesus made it clear to Peter that he wasn't acting out of love for the Lord; rather, he was thinking about himself and how Christ's death would affect him. Paradoxically, Peter's good intentions weren't motivated by love but emanated from Satan. Jesus turned to Peter and said, "Get behind me, Satan! You are a stumbling block to Me; for you are not setting your mind on God's interests but man's" (Matt. 16:23).

As we make choices, we must be certain that we are setting our minds on God's interests, not man's, and that we are motivated by love. Too often, we do something without thinking about why we're doing it. We respond to circumstances or external pressures, just as Peter did, or we do what is expedient and convenient for the moment. Each choice we make should be thoughtfully evaluated and each decision carefully questioned: "Am I truly doing this out of love?" Many times when we examine our motives, we're forced to pull back because we find we're doing something for selfish or wrong reasons. Love restrains us: It keeps us from doing right and good things for the wrong reasons.

Successful life management incorporates the God Factor of love when making choices. Every choice, large or small, limited or far-reaching—from what to serve for dinner to whether to buy a new house—should be grounded in love. God *is* love. The choices we make and the way we execute them should reflect the presence and influence of His love in our lives.

Methods Matter, Too

We need to determine how to implement our choices in God-honoring ways. What would be the most loving course of action for everyone, ourselves included? Sometimes the choices we make may hurt someone, but that is not the same as making hurtful choices.

I remember a time when I had to break off a relationship with a friend. I met her when she attended one of the Bible studies I was teaching. She came to me for counseling, and I ended up discipling her. We spent a lot of time together—shopping, redoing her wardrobe, redecorating her house, pondering the Word. After a while, I realized she was becoming totally dependent on me, instead of becoming more self-reliant, to the extent that she would ask my opinion before she made even the simplest decision. She was phoning me two or three times a day and beginning to resent my other friendships. I tried talking to her: I told her we'd have to spend less time together. She said she understood, but nothing changed.

After a great deal of prayer and talking things over with George and a pastor friend, I decided I had to sever the relationship. My choice hurt her deeply, but it was a loving, not a hurtful, choice. With me out of the picture, she found she could stand on her own feet. She grew and took charge of her life. She learned to lean more fully on the Lord, instead of relying on me.

Methods matter to God. The world purports that the end justifies the means; Christ taught the opposite. Why and how we do something is just as important as the result. His approach was, "What will a man be profited, if he gains the whole world, and forfeits his soul?" (Matt. 16:26). Paul instructed the church at Corinth to "let all things be done properly and in an orderly manner" (1 Cor. 14:40). As Christians, we must be concerned with the manner in which we execute each and every choice.

Consider the Ramifications

Finally, we need to consider the ramifications when making choices. What will the results of our choices be and how will they affect others?

For example, everything I do affects George, because he is my husband. When I make choices, I have to think about how they will reflect on and affect him. As a mother, I must consider what's best for my children. I cannot issue directives or discipline them solely for my personal comfort or convenience. Christians are obligated to apply God's standards when making choices. We may not use life management as a license for doing anything we please.

The world contends that we should look out for #1, think first and, in most cases, exclusively of ourselves. God's way is to "not *merely* look out for your own personal interests, but also for the interests of others" (Phil. 2:4). The God Factor creates a healthy balance between the two.

CREATIVE, CONSTRUCTIVE CHANGES

The God Factor enters into the changes we make as we start managing our lives and time. One of the most formidable tasks we face is deciding what to change and how to change it. Devising and making changes takes a great deal of creativity. We can make alterations but, left to our own devices, how beneficial or enduring they will be is anybody's guess. We need *perspective, a plan, and a purpose* to make effective, appropriate changes. That's where the Lord enters into the process. In the beginning, God created and He hasn't stopped since. He has a plan for each of us. He can show us how to make constructive, creative changes. Before we make any changes, we need to assess our lives and the way we use our time from God's perspective.

When I was in college, one of the requirements in a child development course was to do twelve hours of observation in a preschool. I sat where I could see the children but they couldn't see me, selected one child, and observed him for an hour each session. I was required to keep a diary of everything that happened, recorded exclusively from that child's point of view; that is, I ignored what motivated the teachers, what methods they used, or what the other children did to the child. I was to concentrate solely on what the child did, said, felt, and thought. I remember the professor's exact instructions, because I still have the note-book where I wrote them: "I want you to *be* that child. Look at and react to everything that's said or done from his perspective." That *child's-eye* view taught me a great deal about how differently, and sometimes erroneously, each of us looks at life.

God sees our lives very differently, more clearly and realistically, than we see them. Perhaps you can look at yourself objectively; I can't. I don't think many of us can. We need God's creative assessment of our status quo before we can decide what changes to make.

CAUTIOUS CONTROL

Gaining and maintaining control of our lives may be the most demanding part of self-management. Numerous people own bits and pieces of us. But as Richard Evans observed, "It isn't always others who enslave us. Sometimes we let circumstances enslave us; sometimes we let routines enslave us; sometimes we let things enslave us; sometimes, with weak wills, we enslave ourselves."[2]

Some of us *do* enslave ourselves. We're conditioned to be passive: We let things happen to us, instead of initiating and making things happen for us. Once we decide to take charge of our lives, we have to reverse that process and reclaim our time and our territory. We have to stop succumbing to circumstances or letting others unduly influence us. We have to start making decisions and begin to say no. Sometimes, we have to shift directions, change our opinions, do things differently.

Doing all of those things in the flesh would turn us into power-crazed, self-centered tyrants. In his book *Be Free,* Warren W. Wiersbe noted that although we are free in Christ to be nonconformists, "there is a wrong kind of individualism that destroys instead of fulfills."[3] It's easy, once we start taking control of our lives, to get reckless. Power is a heady commodity.

I know a woman who, for the first forty years of her life, was literally a fixture in other people's lives. She was Lucille's daughter, Henry's wife, Bob and Doris' mother, and everyone's friend. When I first met her, one of her greatest fears was that she might make somebody angry if she disagreed with him or stated her opinion.

Gradually, after she came to know the Lord, her feelings of self-worth improved. She realized she was a person in her own right. Her feelings, opinions, and needs were as valid as anyone else's. For the first time in her life, she started relating to herself. She was as excited as a child with a new toy when she told me, "I've never thought about myself before. It's fun!"

Then, my friend did what many people do when they make a major lifestyle change: She went too far the other way. She, as the saying goes, "let it all hang out." She systematically set out to tell off every person who had ever used or offended her. She said she was through worrying about what other people thought. Her poor husband was completely bewildered when she informed him that keeping house had never fulfilled her, so she was going to get a job and he'd have to help with the housework. Her children, although grown, felt as if they'd lost a mother and gained a stranger.

Fortunately as her needs have been met, she has mellowed; however, in taking charge of her life she did some unnecessary, hurtful things. She equated finding herself with dismissing the feelings of others.

Individualism does not have to be synonymous with inconsideration and selfishness. The apostle Paul certainly was one of the most rugged individualists in Scripture. Yet he was a tender, caring, considerate man who totally expended himself on behalf of the cause of Christ and his brothers and sisters in the faith. "In a society accustomed to interchanging parts, it is good to meet a man like Paul who dared to be himself in the will of God," says Warren Wiersbe.[4]

Taking charge of your life is actually daring to be yourself *in the will of God.* It begins with self-control. Someone can tell you what you should believe, but you can control how you assimilate and apply information. Someone may tell you what he thinks you should do, but you can control your actions. Someone may make you angry, but you can choose how to handle that anger. By exercising self-control, you can also exert a great deal of influence over others and your circumstances. For example, if you are angry, and you use that "soft answer" that turns away wrath instead of screaming at someone, you can influence his response and perhaps prevent a verbal battle.

Interestingly, self-control is one of the fruits of the Spirit, so it is not something we can generate ourselves. God, who is sovereign, enables us to become self-determining individuals. For example, it is God's will that we be kind, so we have to let Him show us how to say no without being nasty. It is His will that we be gracious, so we need to learn how to assert ourselves without being hurtful or abrasive. It is His will that we be truthful, so we need to be able to reject someone's opinion without demeaning him. He teaches us how to gain control of our lives in acceptable ways.

GOD IN MOTION

A word of caution. None of us knows from one minute to the next what's going to happen. Making plans and setting boundaries is good and necessary, but God is in motion in our lives, too, and frequently, within His sovereign will, He does some rearranging.

When Jesus was teaching Nicodemus about the Holy Spirit, He indicated that *being led by the Spirit of the living God will generate unpredictable activity in our lives.* He said that the moving of the Spirit is like the wind: We don't know where it comes from or where it is going but we feel and see its effects. Life management includes being flexible enough to take advantage of this God-initiated activity. We need to realize that sometimes the Lord changes directions in midstream when He asks us to alter plans, shift priorities, and do things we might never think of on our own. His change of direction is all part of His exceeding abundance to us.

Look at how Jesus called the disciples. Simon and Andrew were casting a net into the sea when the Lord walked by and said, " 'Follow Me.' And they immediately left the nets and followed Him" (Mark 1:17–18).

The Lord walked a little farther and came upon James and John who were in a boat mending their nets. "And immediately He called them; and they left their father Zebedee in the boat with the hired servants, and went away to follow Him" (Mark 1:20).

None of them said, "But I'm a fisherman. I can't do what you're asking." No one said, "I'll be with you as soon as I finish what I'm doing." Each was flexible and knew God was in motion in his life and that God's leading superseded all other schedules, plans, or goals.

Being too structured can thwart the movement of the Spirit in our lives. Following His lead helps us walk by faith rather than relying on our own schemes, perfectly planned to the last detail. Martin Baxbaum tells a story that illustrates how being too prepared or trying to exercise too much control can stifle God's moving in our lives and interfere with our walk of faith.

> A chicken-hearted knight had to go on a long journey, so he tried to anticipate all problems. He carried a sword and armor in case he met someone unfriendly, a large jar of ointment for sunburn and poison ivy, an ax for chopping firewood, a tent, blankets, pots and pans, and oats for his horse. He rode off—clanking, gurgling, thudding and tinkling; he was a moving junk pile.
>
> When he was halfway across a dilapidated bridge, the boards gave way and he and his horse fell into the river and drowned because they were so weighted down with unnecessary objects. And, the knight had forgotten to pack a life preserver, which was the one thing he needed most.
>
> The moral of the story is "that he who travels with faith, travels lightest and safest." We can overburden ourselves by being too prepared.[5]

Remembering that God is constantly in motion in our lives helps us manage them well. It also frees us to enjoy that which is ours in Christ without becoming too restrictive or rigid.

JOYOUS ENJOYMENT

At the same time, we must be careful not to misuse that precious freedom we have in Christ. Paul warned, "You

were called to freedom, brethren; only do not turn your
freedom into an opportunity for the flesh" (Gal. 5:13).
We've already established that Christ wants us to possess and
experience full joy and to savor and enjoy life, but there is a
difference between liberty and license. The God Factor helps
us differentiate between them. We must pursue pleasure
within the boundaries the Lord has established. In *Catch a
Red Leaf,* Gladis and Gordon DePree observed: "Being free
to follow my own heart and imagination is a necessary
ingredient in creative living. But when I choose to live
creatively, I must look carefully to the *quality* of my heart
and imagination. In order to live by them, I must have a
heart firmly anchored to God, and an imagination that leads
me in the direction of beauty and light and love."[6]

God is holy—sacred and separate from all that is evil. We
must not seek enjoyment from anything that is sinful or
detracts from His holiness. God is beauty. We should not
derive pleasure from anything that taints His majesty and
splendor. Sometimes, more by default than intent, we let
impurity and ugliness weave their way into our humor or
entertainment and become incorporated into our lives. We
need to keep the Lord's holiness and beauty always before us
as a reminder that our enjoyment is in and through Him. He
must be the initial and predominant source of our pleasure.

Clearly, we cannot properly manage our lives and our
time without the God Factor. It makes the difference
between living and existing and adds spiritual depth and
dimension to every aspect of self-management.

WORKSHOP

I. Write a character sketch depicting God as you know Him. What does your description reveal about your relationship with Him? If you read your sketch to someone who doesn't know the Lord, what impression of Him would it make on her heart?

II. It's time to examine the God Factor in your life-management situation.

1. Think of a choice you made within the last week, then fill in the blanks.
   a. Describe the choice in a few sentences.

   b. What were your motives for choosing as you did?

   c. Describe the method you used in executing the choice.

   d. List everyone who was directly or indirectly affected by your choice and tell how they were affected.

   e. If you could do it over, what would you change, if anything?

f. Write a paragraph telling how the God Factor of love influenced your choosing.

2. Answer each of the following questions, incorporating the God Factor of creativity. Pray. Listen to the Lord. Let your thoughts flow.
   a. Write five sentences telling how you feel about yourself.

   b. What constructive changes do you think the Lord would have you make in yourself?

   c. Write five sentences telling how you feel about your life.

   d. Where should you begin to revamp your life?

e. What are three specific things you can do to become the person God wants you to be?

f. List three changes you want to make in your life. Tell the purpose for each and what results you might expect from the changes.

3. Are you daring to be yourself in the will of God? Describe or discuss how you could take charge of your life in each of the following situations without being abrasive or rude or without sacrificing your individualism.

a. The superintendent of the Sunday school asks you to teach a class and you don't want to.

b. Your husband announces that the two of you have been invited to go to dinner with his boss and his wife this Thursday evening. He's forgotten that's the night you attend class at the local junior college.

c. A friend disagrees with your stand on a heated political issue and accuses you of being narrow-minded.

d. You've just spent three hours baking cookies for a bake sale at the church, which the president of the missionary society badgered you into doing in the first place, when a committee member calls to tell you they won't be having the sale after all, but thanks anyway.

e. Your hairdresser, who has just completed a course in a new hair-coloring technique, is determined that you should color your hair. She has just spent ten minutes telling you why you should have it done.

f. You and your husband have agreed to let your teenage son (or daughter) go on a week's vacation with your next-door neighbors, who are not of your faith. You have known the people for years and trust them implicitly. Then, your pastor preaches a sermon on the dangers of maintaining close friendships with unbelievers.

g. You're shopping with a good friend. She tries on and "falls in love with" a dress that looks absolutely awful on her. She asks your opinion. (Remember, it's a sin to tell a lie!)

4. Look up each of the following verses, then write a God Factor of wisdom that is described in it.

a. Proverbs 2:3

b. Proverbs 3:35

c. Proverbs 9:8

d. Proverbs 9:9, 10:14

e. Proverbs 12:15, 19:20

f. Proverbs 14:16

g. Proverbs 14:33; 17:24

h. Proverbs 15:24; 24:14

i. Proverbs 24:5

j. Proverbs 2:6–7

5. Read Acts 8:1–3, 9:1–30 to see what happened to Paul when God was in motion in his life. Next, describe in your own words how his experience illustrates the necessity for flexibility.

6. Look up each of the following passages and summarize what it says about how we can incorporate the God Factors of holiness and beauty into our lives.

    a. Proverbs 23:20–21

    b. Proverbs 22:24–25

    c. Romans 16:19b

    d. 1 Corinthians 10:31

    e. 2 Corinthians 6:14

    f. Ephesians 4:29

    g. Ephesians 5:3–4

    h. Philippians 4:8

Chapter Three

THE BASICS OF SELF-DISCIPLINE

"Like a city that is broken into and without walls is a man who has no control over his spirit" (Proverbs 25:28).

I could tell by the sound of her voice that Sandy was on the verge of tears when she phoned. "You'll never guess what I just did."

"What?" I asked hesitantly, dreading the answer.

"I just blew a trip to London. Don has to go there for a weeklong business trip. He told me last night if I could get ready by this evening, I could go." She burst into tears. "There's no way. My life is such a mess. I can't even find my passport. My raincoat is filthy. I never got around to taking it to the cleaners last fall after I dropped it in the mud at the football field. I have nine loads of laundry to do because I got sidetracked Friday making the decorations for the mother-daughter banquet, and those aren't finished either because Jean and I never got back to them after we went for lunch. The Broadway was having a storewide sale and . . . Anyway, the banquet is the Saturday after I'd get back on Friday, and the decorations and placecards *have* to be done, and I still haven't found anyone to do the music. I don't know what's the matter with me! I can't seem to do anything right."

Sound like anyone you know? Sandy's problem isn't that she's incompetent: She's a very talented, capable woman. It isn't that she's disorganized: She's great at chairing committees and planning programs. Sandy's problem is a common one: She isn't self-disciplined. Consequently, her life *is* a mess, a constant maze of unending pressures and unfinished tasks. She does a great deal but accomplishes very little, and she misses out on many good things, such as spur-of-the-moment trips to London or the simple pleasure of having time to herself. Sandy needs to learn self-control.

Solomon, in his wisdom, compared a person who lacks discipline to a city whose walls are broken down: "like a city that is broken into and without walls is a man who has no control over his spirit" (Prov. 25:28). In biblical times, cities were fortified with walls, perhaps twenty-feet thick and over twenty-five feet high, to keep enemies out. Soldiers constantly stood guard on top of the walls, so they could see in all directions for miles. What walls did for cities, self-control does for the human spirit. It fortifies and protects us as well as makes us strong. H. A. Ironside stated, "Self mastery is the greatest of all victories. Self-control is ever important. This is the temperance of the New Testament."[1]

Self-management starts with *self,* not with management. We have to learn to control ourselves before we can alter our actions or circumstances and take charge of our lives. Life management isn't accomplished by changing the things we do. It begins when we change ourselves, our attitudes, and our approach to life.

WHAT IS SELF-DISCIPLINE?

Self-discipline is the foundation for and the core of life management. Each of us has his own idea of what self-discipline is. Bill Vaughan, in the *Kansas City Star,* said, "Discipline is like broccoli. We may not care for it ourselves, but feel sure it would be good for everybody else." W. K. Hope noted that "Self-discipline is when your conscience tells you to do something and you don't talk back." The word discipline has its origin in the verb disciple, meaning to learn.

When we were children, we were *other* disciplined. Our

parents and family, teachers, coaches, and other adults maintained jurisdiction over certain areas of our lives. As we matured, we were expected to take responsibility for our own behavior. As Paul said, we are to "grow up in all aspects into [Christ]" (Eph. 4:15).

Children are wishy-washy, unable to control themselves or their thoughts. They are "tossed here and there by waves" of circumstance (Eph. 4:14). Refusing to discipline ourselves is the same as saying that we want to live like children. We would rather let external forces batter us around like a cork in the sea than use internal motivation to direct and control our lives.

There are five basics to understand for developing self-discipline: the importance of self-discipline, the impact of the will, the instinct of work, the impossibility of perfection, and the investment of time. We'll discuss the first two basics in this chapter and the other three in the next.

THE IMPORTANCE OF SELF-DISCIPLINE

Self-discipline makes the difference between running our lives or having them run us because it is the way we gain and maintain control. As we train ourselves to do what needs to be done methodically and regularly, chaos and confusion subside. We are able to accomplish the things we want to accomplish and also free up large portions of time. As we discipline ourselves to think properly, we gain peace of mind because our thoughts are no longer agitated with worry, fear, or frustration. As we develop principles to live by and learn how to express emotions in acceptable ways, we become calmer and more confident. We take charge of our lives.

A self-disciplined person handles little details thoroughly and well as they occur, thereby controlling the *big picture*. Think about the things that almost kept Sandy from going to London. (Yes, some of us bailed her out: Don found her passport in the filing cabinet in the den; I loaned her my raincoat and helped her do laundry and pack; Linda took over as chairperson of the entertainment committee and promised to see that everything got done; her neighbor offered to take care of the children until her parents could drive down from Fresno to baby-sit; and another friend who is a hairdresser worked her in for a quick appointment.) If Sandy had taken a few minutes when she went grocery shopping or ran errands to drop her coat at the cleaners, it would have been ready to wear when she needed it. If she'd done a load of laundry every day, she and her family would have had clean clothes. If she'd scheduled a time to make the decorations and forced herself to stick to the job until it was done, she and her committee could have finished everything in one day. If she'd forced herself to pick up the phone and call someone to do the music, if she and Jean hadn't gone out to lunch or hadn't gone shopping instead of making placecards—*if* Sandy would have handled little details thoroughly and well as they had occurred, she would have been running her life, not vice-versa. Self-discipline is the key to gaining and maintaining control of your life.

Winning Over Your Will

Self-discipline is also important because it helps us do God's will. Jesus said, "If anyone wishes to come after Me, let him deny himself, and take up his cross, and follow Me" (Matt. 16:24). Self-discipline is a positive, constructive form of self-denial. Self-discipline helps us say no to ourselves and yes to God whenever "the flesh sets its desire against the Spirit" (Gal. 5:17). Then, we resist temptation and choose God's will over ours. Self-denial is never easy, but it is certainly beneficial.

A month ago, I initiated Operation Swimsuit, the diet and intensified exercise program I do every spring to take off that extra ten or so pounds that accumulate during the winter. Sweets put and keep weight on me faster than any other kind of food, so the diet I use eliminates *all* sugar, even fruit for the first month. I can't describe how extremely difficult it was to wash grapes and luscious, big, red strawberries or cut sweet, yummy cantaloupe during the first couple of weeks. I wished I could put my entire family on my diet, so I wouldn't have to have any fresh fruit in the house. But the most difficult test came when I had to bake a batch of homemade oatmeal cookies. I actually had to leave the kitchen to keep from munching them when they were fresh and warm from the oven. But I forced myself not to eat even one bite because I knew one would lead to a handful.

Later after the cookies were safely tucked away in the cookie jar, I felt good. Knowing I'd maintained control over my appetite was worth missing a cookie (or the ten I'd normally have eaten).

Self-discipline Equals Accomplishment

Self-discipline is also important because it helps us accomplish what we want to accomplish. It takes us from step A to step B to step C. The apostle Paul compared the "game of life" to a race and observed that "everyone who competes in the game exercises self-control in all things" (1 Cor. 9:25).

As a free-lance writer I'm essentially self-employed. I pick and choose what I write and when I write it. Several months ago, I contracted with Zondervan to write this book. I have a specific calendar deadline. No one from the publishing house has ever called and asked if I'm working on the manuscript, nor has my editor phoned to inquire what chapter I'm writing. Nevertheless, I'm employed by them. I have to discipline myself to walk down the back hallway in my home every morning, close the door to my office, and set pencil to paper.

Some days, I'm really up for it. It's a joy and delight to write when sharp ideas hang on the tip of my mind and the words flow onto paper. But on the days when my brain is as creative as a block of cement and when everything I write sounds like it's been written before—in a first grade reader—I'd much rather skip out and sit by the pool, sew, garden, or go shopping and to lunch with a friend, but I can't. I'd never finish a manuscript unless I disciplined myself. And if I didn't, I would never experience the tremendous sense of satisfaction and accomplishment that accompanies holding a book with my name on it, knowing God will in some way use it for His honor and glory.

Self-discipline contributes to accomplishment because it helps us set, work toward, and attain goals—it gives focus to our lives. Goals are no more than useless daydreams unless they are implemented. James Allen, author of *As a Man Thinketh,* wrote, "They who have no central purpose in their life fall an easy prey to petty worries, fears, troubles, and self-pitying, all of which lead . . . to failure, unhappiness, and loss."[2]

THE IMPACT OF THE WILL

A second basic we must understand to achieve self-discipline is *the impact of the will.* Will is a wish or desire combined with determination. We have already discussed how we are created in the image of God. He has a will and subsequently created humankind with volition. Each of us is endowed with the God-instilled ability to make choices. We are not push-button robots controlled by chance or circumstances or even by a master switch labeled *God.* James Allen observed: "Man . . . contains within himself that transforming and regenerative agency by which he may make of himself what he will."[3] You can, by an act of your will, exert control over yourself and your circumstances and choose to become self-disciplined. *If you are not self-disciplined as an adult, it isn't because you cannot learn how or because of the way you were raised but because you have chosen not to be. That is your will concerning self-discipline.*

Our wills influence everything we do: the thoughts we

think, the actions we take, the feelings we express. To achieve self-discipline, we must admit that our wills may be what keep us from that goal. Let's examine how we can choose to become self-disciplined and how we can submit our wills to God's will and let Him mold them for our best interests.

Acknowledge Sin

First, we must *acknowledge that our wills have been tainted by sin*. Consequently, we are going to want to do things that we shouldn't do and not want to do the things we should. Paul struggled with this impact of will. He said, "For that which I am doing, I do not understand; for I am not practicing what I would like to do . . . the good that I wish, I do not do" (Rom. 7:15, 19).

Wanting to be self-disciplined is not enough. Desire must be coupled with determination and a reliance on God. The only way to eradicate the taint of sin from your will is by acknowledging its presence and then asking Christ to remove it. Paul rejoiced that our Lord Jesus Christ can free the will from sin. (See Rom. 7:24–25.)

I'm Willful; I Admit It

The second step in learning to control the will is to *admit when we're being willful*. We have to stop making excuses about why we aren't self-disciplined.

When I teach the topic of self-management, I get a lot of feedback from women explaining why they haven't taken charge of their lives or time. Some seem compelled to come to me or write to me and explain why they aren't self-disciplined, as if I'd know whether or not they are. One excuse I hear frequently is "I'm not naturally that way. I'm a very unstructured person, and that's the way God made me." In other words, some people blame the Lord for their lack of self-discipline.

Another common excuse is that self-discipline is too

restrictive. One woman told me she was afraid that exercising self-control would hamper the moving of the Spirit in her life. Another claimed she was easy-going and didn't want to "ruin" her personality. The most amusing excuse was offered by a woman who said, "I've always wanted to be self-disciplined but I'm so busy, I just haven't gotten around to it." The most frustrating comments come from women who say they *can't* discipline themselves; the most encouraging are from those who say they don't know how but would like to learn. At least, they want to change.

Each and every excuse we make about why we aren't or can't be self-disciplined is actually a refusal to admit we're being willful. We need to be honest with ourselves if we are going to control our will: We must admit that lack of self-discipline is a personal choice in which we exert our will.

Hand It Over to God

Third, you can reshape your will by *asking the Lord to take charge of it*—hand it over to God. Jesus understands each of our struggles. He battled against His human desire in Gethsemane. He literally presented His will to the Father through prayer. First, He stated His will, "If it is possible, let this cup pass from Me . . ." Next, He asked the Father to reshape His will if what He had asked disagreed with God's will. He said, "Yet, not as I will, but as Thou wilt" (Matt. 26:39).

This change of will didn't come easily, even for Christ. He labored in prayer for several hours until His will conformed to the Father's. "He was praying very fervently; and His sweat became like drops of blood, falling down upon the ground" (Luke 22:44).

Conforming our will to God's will isn't simple. It takes persistence and prayer. We can do this by following Christ's example. First, we need to state our wills to the Father. Next, we need to discern God's will by asking Him to reveal it to us. Then, we need to submit our will to His if there is a conflict between the two: We need to hand our will over to God.

Tell Yourself No

Finally, the will can be reshaped by *acting in opposition to it*. Deny yourself! Exert will power! Make yourself stick to your plans. Do what you have to do whether or not you want to. Don't give up when everything within you is urging you to. Start saying no to yourself, no matter how badly you want to say yes. Start doing what needs to be done. Stop procrastinating!

PROCRASTINATION

Procrastination is putting off until tomorrow, or the next day, or the day after that what should have been done yesterday, or the day before, or last week. It is to avoid doing what's distasteful or inconvenient at the moment. Procrastination originates from a lack of self-discipline—both mental and physical discipline.

Physical procrastination is simply not doing. Mental procrastination is thinking of what *not* to do—how to ignore, by-pass, or get out of doing something—instead of thinking of what to do and how to do it. Lord Chesterfield observed, "Idleness is only the refuge of weak minds, and the holiday of fools." Contriving ways to put off doing something may afford a momentary "holiday," but ignoring work and responsibility doesn't remove them. If you leave the dishes in the sink, they'll still be there in the morning. If you don't type that report, it won't write itself. Thinking up ways to procrastinate takes as much time and sometimes more effort and creativity than facing up to a job and doing it.

God's View of Procrastination

Solomon penned a revealing portrait of a procrastinator in Proverbs. Let's study the characteristics of a procrastinator as seen from God's point of view. "I went by the field of the slothful, and by the vineyard of the man void of understanding; and, lo, it was all grown over with thorns, and nettles had covered the face thereof, and the stone wall thereof was broken down" (Prov. 24:30–31 KJV).

We see that procrastinators are "void of understanding." They don't use common sense. Instead of taking that stitch in time that saves nine, they wait until an entire garment unravels. They make more, not less, work for themselves by procrastinating.

Solomon tells us procrastinators are "slothful." In Scripture, the word "slothful" means dull or unresponsive, referring to an animal, the sloth, that lives only in the dense interior of the forest. Sloths are so handicapped that their survival is threatened if they venture out to face new frontiers. Being very low in intelligence and moving very slowly, only fourteen feet per hour, they are the retardates of the animal world. That means it would take one of them sixty minutes to walk through the average family room.

So, they drag about, barely moving and quite unaware of what's going on around them. Their greatest pleasure comes from sleeping, usually about eighteen hours out of every twenty-four. When faced with danger or attacked, they can only passively defend themselves by relying solely on their thick fur for protection because they neither fight back nor run away.

The Word of God likens procrastinators to sloths. Like sloths, procrastinators are hemmed in and limited by the dense interior of their disorganized, chaotic lives. They survive but don't enjoy life as God intended. They cannot handle any new project because they haven't handled the old one(s) because they are generally lazy, love sleeping or napping, move slowly, and have little mental or physical stamina. And when faced with emergencies, criticism, or needs, they have no defenses. Instead, they stand helpless and vulnerable because they rely on unacceptable excuses to explain away failures and frustrations.

Go to the Ant

In Proverbs 6:6–8, Solomon used the example of another of God's creatures to extol the virtues of self-discipline: "Go to the ant, thou sluggard; consider her ways, and be wise: Which having no guide, overseer, or ruler, Provideth her meat in the summer, and gathereth her food in the harvest" (KJV). The ant, who exemplifies a self-disciplined person, is wise. She's self-motivated so nobody has to tell her what to do. She consistently does what must be done. She plans ahead and provides for herself: She's prepared. Procrastinators, on the other hand, sit back, put up their feet, slip their brains into neutral, and wait until the last possible moment to do anything. They're always ready to grab a nap.

After describing the dilapidated conditions caused by procrastination, Solomon said, "When I saw, I reflected upon it; I looked at [the vineyard that was all grown over with thorns and nettles and the broken down stone wall], and received instruction. A little sleep, a little slumber, a little folding of the hands to rest: then your poverty will come like a robber; and your want like an armed man" (Prov. 24:32–34). Procrastination has dire results. One is a confused, disorderly life that is all grown over with the effects of inactivity and lack of concern. Another is poverty. I believe this is a poverty of spirit, as well as money and possessions, because idleness, laziness, and negligence detract from dignity and deplete our feelings of self-worth. All in all, procrastinators lead unproductive lives.

How to Overcome Procrastination

Lack of productivity is both the *cause* and the *result* of procrastination. We aren't productive because we procrastinate, and when we procrastinate, we don't produce. The only way to stop procrastinating is to start performing. We have to discipline ourselves to do what needs to be done when it should be done. For sporadic procrastinators, that won't be too difficult.

Most of us periodically procrastinate in some way. I hate to take the time to get gas in my car, so I always wait until the low-fuel light goes on before I pull into a service station. George hates to shop, so he always waits until his entire wardrobe is falling apart before he goes to the store to buy new clothes. (Actually, I drag him.)

However, overcoming procrastination isn't easy for people who do it habitually. It will require concentrated effort and a definite plan of action. Here are ten steps that will help even the most adept "putter-offers" conquer procrastination. Remember, reading them won't help; you have to do them.

Step One: *Do something.* Most procrastinators are so accustomed to not doing that they can't get going even when they want to. Even simple acts generate momentum. Activity alleviates apathy by getting you involved in the task at hand. When you begin to work on overcoming procrastination, don't worry about what to do first, or you'll sit down to think about it and end up doing nothing. Just attack some project or responsibility you've neglected. Throw your heart and body into it and don't stop until it's finished. Follow Paul's advice: "Whatever you do, do your work heartily, as for the Lord" (Col. 3:23).

Step Two: *Commit every task—large or small, important or menial—to the Lord.* Solomon counseled, "Commit your works to the Lord, and your plans will be established" (Prov. 16:3). You need to involve Christ in everything you do. You cannot overcome faults and failings by yourself, "but in all these things [you] overwhelmingly conquer through Him who loved [you]" (Rom. 8:37).

Step Three: *Do it now.* Take charge of your life by refusing to procrastinate. Putting off what has to be done doesn't make sense because ignoring obligations and duties doesn't delete them; rather, it compounds them until you're faced with a monumental task, instead of a simple chore.

The Lord taught that "each day has enough trouble of its own" (Matt. 6:34). Don't create problems where none would exist if you didn't procrastinate. Most crises are preventable. If you wait to handle an incident until the worst happens, you've probably gone beyond the point of no return. Instead of waiting, train yourself to foresee potential problems. Prevent them rather than reacting to situations once they surface.

Use your will power. Promise yourself that just for today, you will handle every single responsibility *as it arises.* When you make it through a day and discover how much you've accomplished, you'll be motivated to do the same thing tomorrow.

Step Four: *Stop making excuses for yourself.* Instead of saying you're not doing something because you don't have time, or don't know how, or hate to, or are too tired, or have better things to do, admit that you are procrastinating. Every time you make a "doing excuse" say, "I'm procrastinating." Then, channel your creativity toward accomplishing a task instead of dreaming up ways to delay doing it.

Step Five: *Don't do to keep from doing.* Procrastination isn't always sitting around doing nothing. Sometimes, it's doing one thing to avoid doing another. For example, you might do gardening to keep from making business calls. You may make unnecessary business calls to keep from finishing that report you didn't want to write. Don't substitute an unnecessary activity for one that needs to be done, even though it may seem like you aren't procrastinating.

Step Six: *Do the worst first.* We have a tendency to put off the things we least like or don't enjoy doing. They're always hovering in the background, so we build psychological barriers against them and avoid them as long as we possibly can. We can successfully combat procrastination by tackling those distasteful tasks first. Once they're out of the way, we can look forward to doing activities we enjoy.

Step Seven: *Do it well.* "Whatever your hand finds to do, verily, do it with all your might" (Eccl. 9:10). Richelieu exhorted, "Carry on every enterprise as if all depended on the success of it." People tend to procrastinate on mundane, repetitive, thankless, never-ending tasks because much of the ordinary work we do is boring or gets undone as quickly as it gets done. Things like pulling weeds, doing laundry, washing the car, and alphabetizing and filing reports aren't exactly fun, but they contribute to our comfort, pleasure, and achievements. There's usually something distasteful in any task no matter how pleasant the overall job is.

As you start performing, remember that doing isn't sufficient; you need to do your best. My sister-in-law Dorothy, who passed away several years ago, was an outstanding cook. She could put together a delicious meal and get in and out of the kitchen in record time. I was surprised when she once told me she hated to cook. Her strategy? Since she disliked cooking, she'd learned to do it quickly and well, so she wasn't miserable every time she had to fix a meal. I recommend that approach to you. Develop skills for the things you have to do. Find the simplest, easiest ways to tackle your chores. Concentrate on what you're doing, instead of thinking about how much you dislike doing it. Be zealous about whatever you do.

Step Eight: *Educate yourself.* Learning how to do things well is important because you tend to put off things you can't do. Socrates wrote, "Whom, then, do I call educated? First, those who manage well the circumstances which they encounter day by day; and those who possess a judgment which is accurate in meeting occasions as they arise and rarely miss the expedient course of action."

The easiest way to learn how to do something is to have someone adept at it show you how to do it, step-by-step. When I got my word-processing program, I spent several weeks sifting through pages of complicated instructions, which sounded as if they were written in a foreign language, and then trying each procedure on the computer. Last night, a young man from our church, who is a writer, came over to see how my program worked because he was thinking of buying one. I sat at the keyboard and in fifteen minutes showed him how to do what had taken me weeks to learn. The best way to train yourself to do things is by imitating someone who knows how. Education develops efficiency and expediency and helps us overcome procrastination.

Step Nine: *Develop positive-performance habits.* Columnist Frank A. Clark defined a "habit" as "something you can do without thinking, which is why most of us have so many of them." Monta Crane observed, "The worst boss anyone can have is a bad habit." Procrastination *is* bad, and it *is* a habit: a learned response that can be unlearned.

If you're going to overcome procrastination, you need to think differently about approaching responsibility. Then, modify your behavior: Decide what you want to change and devise specific steps you will take to alter your performance. Don't try to change your entire life at once. Start with one habit you want to change. Consider its negative effects. Concentrate on developing a *new* habit rather than replacing an old one.

For example, if you consistently oversleep and refuse to drag yourself out of bed until the last possible moment, you first need to survey the costly consequences of sleeping in. You start the day with a hassle. Chaos is the established pattern. People miss breakfast. Children go to school too emotionally distraught to think well. You're so frazzled you feel like you've been in a marathon race by the time you get to the office or are ready to tackle the household chores.

Next, to break the procrastination habit, decide precisely what you need to do to force yourself out of bed earlier every morning and give full attention to it. Don't dwell on the half-hour of sleep you're missing. Think about how quiet the house is. Enjoy the dawn. Focus on each thing you do, such as packing lunches or shaving. Get engrossed in pleasant positives.

When you first start deprograming the procrastination habit, don't make any exceptions. If you've procrastinated about starting an exercise program but have now decided to walk thirty minutes every day, do it come hail or high water, sore muscles or a phone call from a friend. Remember, you're nurturing a new way of doing and responding.

Step Ten: *Reward yourself.* Scripture teaches that work is its own reward: "In all labor there is profit" (Prov. 14:23). But if you're like most people, you like to receive some tangible token of appreciation. Don't make the mistake of expecting everyone to praise you for your efforts. You may get compliments when your family, friends, and associates notice changes, but consider their favorable responses an unexpected blessing. Reward *yourself* for a job well done. Settle down with a cup of tea and make a phone call to a friend after you've cleaned the hall closet you've been ignoring for five years. Buy a new dress when you've lost ten pounds. Treat yourself to a manicure or pedicure at your favorite salon for keeping the house clean and not letting the laundry pile up for a whole week. Get tickets to the ball game as a reward for cleaning the garage. You deserve it! You've worked hard!

WORKSHOP

I. How self-disciplined are you? This quiz will help you decide. Write the appropriate word in the blank: always, usually, sometimes, seldom, never. If you have too many *seldom* or *never* answers, list one thing you can do to correct the problem.

    1. I handle little details thoroughly and well as they occur. _____

    2. I say no to myself when necessary. _____

    3. I am working toward and accomplishing goals. _____

    4. I try to mold my will to God's will. _____

    5. I am willing to admit when I am being willful. _____

    6. I want to be self-disciplined. _____

    7. I am developing my capabilities. _____

    8. I have a positive mindset about work. _____

    9. I try new things and absorb new ideas. _____

    10. I invest my time wisely. _____

    11. I would describe myself as a self-disciplined person. _____

    12. My friends and family would describe me as a self-disciplined person. _____

II. What is your procrastination quotient? The following exercise will help you develop a plan to overcome the procrastination habit.

    1. Use a dictionary to find three synonyms for procrastinate.

2. Describe one area where you are mentally undisciplined.

3. List three things you can do to discipline yourself mentally in that area.

4. Describe one area where you are physically undisciplined.

5. List three things you can do to discipline yourself physically in that area.

6. List as many excuses as you can for your procrastinating. Draw a line through any that are not valid.

7. Describe your worst procrastination problem.

8. Outline, step-by-step, a performance procedure you will use to overcome that problem.

9. Write a short prayer committing that task to the Lord.

Chapter Four   DISCIPLINING
                                     YOURSELF

*"Make it your ambition to lead a quiet life and attend to your
own business and work with your hands"* (1 Thess. 4:11).

Discipling ourselves isn't easy. Knowing we're not the
only ones who have faced such struggles is encouraging.
During biblical times, the Thessalonians had a similar
problem. They were wonderful Christians who dearly loved
their Lord. Their example of faith was so outstanding that
Paul praised them repeatedly. But he also admonished them:
"For we hear that some among you are leading an undisciplined life . . ." (2 Thess. 3:11).

Then Paul instructed his brothers and sisters in Christ
about how to discipline themselves. He said, "Make it your
ambition to lead a quiet life and attend to your own business
and work with your hands." Let's explore how to do that.

In the last chapter, we discussed the first two basics in
becoming self-disciplined: the importance of self-discipline
and the impact of the will. We also looked at the various
ways many of us procrastinate rather than act. In this
chapter, we will discuss the other three basics of self-
discipline: the instinct of work, the impossibility of perfection, and the investment of time.

THE INSTINCT OF WORK

Another important basic factor in self-discipline is the
instinct of work. We need to develop positive attitudes about
work. We must accept that it is a natural, normal part of our

godlikeness, an attribute we inherit as a result of being created in the image of God.

Each of us possesses a need to perform, create, and develop our capabilities. This drive was built into us by the Lord. From the beginning, He assigned certain tasks for woman and man to do. He instructed them to "be fruitful and multiply, and fill the earth, and subdue it; and rule over the fish of the sea and over the birds of the sky, and over every living thing that moves on earth" (Gen. 1:28).

Some people believe work is part of the curse, a hex God imposed on humankind to punish us for sin. That is not so. Before Adam and Eve ever sank their teeth into the forbidden fruit, the Lord assigned them jobs. One of Adam's first tasks was to name the animals. In addition, "The Lord God took the man and put him into the garden of Eden to cultivate it and keep it" (Gen. 2:15).

How can we develop a positive mindset about work? First, we can accept that working is normal. Shunning work is going against a God-created instinct. Second, we need to realize that working is good for us. It is physically and emotionally beneficial because it makes us use our brains and bodies. Physical activity actually causes the body to produce chemicals that act as natural tranquilizers and appetite suppressors. St. John Chrysostom said, "Labor is a powerful medicine." So, throwing ourselves into a job can make us forget about our problems. The writer of Proverbs noted that hard work is profitable for more than money; it enriches us intellectually and spiritually: "The soul of the diligent is made fat" (Prov. 13:4).

What You Work for Is What You Get

We need to realize that God has chosen to supply us through work. Work isn't always the norm in our society. A few weeks ago, I read a newspaper article about some teenagers from an economically depressed area who applied for a new summer job program. They were turned away because not one of them knew *how* to work. They didn't understand simple procedures: how to initiate ideas or make plans, accept responsibility, or work in group situations. The reporter concluded that the work ethic has been killed by handouts.

Those youth came from families that had been on welfare for three and four generations. They had no role models who worked, so they had no sense of how to go about earning their keep. Their instinct to work had never been awakened.

Procrastination and lack of self-discipline dull or destroy the work instinct. Paul declared, "If anyone will not work, neither let him eat" (2 Thess. 3:10). Proverbs 13:11 affirms that "one who gathers [wealth] by labor increases it." Another proverb warns that "an idle man will suffer hunger" (Prov. 19:15). In God's economy, we have to sow before we can reap. To become self-disciplined, we must realize and act on the truth that work is a natural, normal, required part of life.

THE IMPOSSIBILITY OF PERFECTION

The fourth basic we must understand concerning self-discipline is *the impossibility of perfection.* To err *is* human. Eric Severeid noted, "Human beings are not perfectible. They *are* improvable." Making mistakes is intrinsic to growth, learning, and life. There is a vast difference between being perfectionistic and being self-disciplined.

Outwardly, perfectionists seem to be extremely self-disciplined, but they actually aren't. Self-disciplined people exert self-control over whatever comes along. They allow for error; they allow for individual differences that don't match their standards. Perfectionists constantly struggle to formulate situations, to control not only themselves but every person or circumstance in their lives. They do not manage their lives well because they're always trying to fit everything and everyone into some preconceived mold.

Monsignor John J. Sullivan once said, "All except the shallowest living involves tearing up one rough draft after another." Perfectionists don't believe in rough drafts; they do everything according to a fixed blueprint of their own making. The problem is, life seldom matches their design.

Perfectionism Destroys Creativity

Let's look at some reasons why perfectionism is so damaging to life management. First, it destroys creativity because it makes you task-oriented. Perfectionists are concerned with doing things a certain way, their *perfect* way, so they concentrate on the process rather than on developing ideas or relating to people. Perfectionists suffer from what I call "fear of trying," so deprive themselves of the opportunity to discover what they can do. Many do not recognize or develop their creative potential because being perfectionistic leaves no room for trial and error, experimentation and change.

Perfectionism Isn't Healthy

Perfectionism is also physically and emotionally unhealthy. Time-management specialist Edwin Bliss points out, "There is a difference between striving for excellence and striving for perfection. The first is attainable, gratifying, and healthy. The second is unattainable, frustrating, and neurotic."[1] Perfectionism takes the pleasure out of accomplishment because perfectionists always wish they had done better. The unrealistic standards they impose upon themselves cause a great deal of stress that engenders physical ailments, such as migraine headaches, ulcers, and high blood pressure. Some doctors link perfectionism to cancer.

Perfectionists seldom, if ever, relax. They force their bodies and minds to work overtime. One of my friends, who is married to a perfectionist, told me her husband actually clenches his fists and grits his teeth in his sleep. Being in control and having to be right sap an inordinate amount of energy.

Because perfection is unattainable, perfectionists become depressed, feel they have failed, and deplete their own self-esteem. In their book *Happiness is a Choice,* Frank B. Minirth, M.D., and Paul D. Meier, M.D., explain, "Out of all the various personality types in our culture, there is one type that is more likely than any other to get depressed sometime in life. Psychiatrists call this type the obsessive-compulsive personality. Most laypersons call him a perfectionist."[2]

For example, Molly is one of the most beautiful women I've ever known—tall, thin, long-waisted, classic high cheekbones, ivory skin. One day when I stopped by to pick her up for a shopping trip, I found her in tears. "I can't go," she sobbed.

"What's wrong?" I asked, certain something terrible had happened.

Her reason? "I look too awful to be seen in public."

I eyed her from head to toe. Except for her smeared mascara, she looked absolutely gorgeous to me, and I told her so. She proceeded to tell me how her hair was sticking out the wrong way, her make-up didn't cover a slight blemish on her chin, the suit she was wearing made her look fat. . . . I can't remember all of her grievances, but nothing I said could convince her of how lovely she looked.

I found out later that Molly "hates" the way she looks. When she and her husband were on a cruise, she stayed in their cabin the night they were asked to sit at the captain's table because she thought she looked ugly. Molly and people like her defeat happiness because they aren't willing to settle for less than perfect.

Perfectionism is self-defeating and breeds inertia. Perfectionists would rather stick with the known, which is easier to control, than to venture into the unknown. They end up stuck in the status quo. They do not manage their lives well, just rigidly, and as a result, waste a lot of time.

A Time Waster

Perfectionism wastes time because it focuses on unnecessary details. There's no way to make everything perfect. One of my friends is such a perfectionist that she won't let anyone help her do dishes. They have to be stacked just so before she carries them to the counter. Each dish has its own special spot in the dishwasher. Cleanup has to be done in a certain order: The table has to be washed before the stove and cupboards. She spends at least forty-five minutes in the kitchen every night after dinner. Her husband and two children are more than happy not to help because even when they do, she criticizes their efforts and redoes the job.

Perfectionists like my friend spend hours trying to do things perfectly. They expend huge amounts of effort and energy trying to make people and situations match their standards of excellence. Time is too precious to waste, especially on empty pursuits like perfectionism.

THE INVESTMENT OF TIME

A fifth basic we need to understand to become self-disciplined is *the investment of time*. Time should neither be wasted nor even consumed, but invested, much like money. Every year George and I put the maximum allowable amount into Individual Retirement Accounts. We originally opened them at our bank because it was convenient. This year our accountant told us we weren't getting the best return for our money. He suggested we switch from fixed-rate to flexible-rate accounts where the interest will be compounded daily instead of quarterly, and he told us to shop around for the highest rates and find the best possible investment.

We need to learn how to invest our time, as well as our money, so we get the greatest return for the minutes and hours God allots us. We have to discipline ourselves to make the most of our time. Basically, we allocate time in one of three ways: We *find* time, *take* time, or *make* time.

Finding Time

Most of us use the *find-time* technique. A major portion of our lives is devoted to established routines: up at 6:30, shower and breakfast, out the door by 7:00, in the office from 8:30 to 5:00, home by 6:30, Bible study on Tuesday nights, bowling on Thursday evenings, golf or yard work on Saturday morning, church on Sunday. When we want to do anything that is not a regular part of our routine, we find time by inserting activities into vacant time slots where something isn't scheduled.

For example, let's say you're asked to serve on the Christian education committee at the church. It meets on the third Monday night each month. You don't do anything on Monday evenings, so you accept. You fill that time slot because it's empty.

Finding time doesn't require self-discipline or thought: You simply use whatever time is available to do whatever comes along. That isn't a wise way to determine time usage. Time, not desire or necessity, becomes the deciding factor in what you do. You agree to serve on the committee because it meets on Monday night when you aren't busy, not because you feel you have something to contribute, or have a burden for the Sunday school, or are convinced it is God's will for you.

Taking Time

Another ineffective approach to time usage is *taking time*. The *take-time* technique involves borrowing time from one area to use in another. People who allocate time this way juggle activities within their crammed schedules because they are already overextended. They don't have time gaps but create them by manipulating their routines.

Susan is a typical "time taker." She is pursuing a modeling

career, so her schedule is very erratic. She never knows when she'll be called for an interview or an assignment. She's a dedicated Christian. She ministers in the college department at her church, which includes teaching a class on Sunday morning plus attending camps and social functions. In addition, she does the normal socializing any young woman her age would do.

Susan never knows from one hour to the next what she'll be doing. One of her friends recently commented that she has "cancelitis." She's forever changing plans at the last minute, is quite unreliable, and generally ends up inconveniencing somebody.

Time takers like Susan are masters at juggling schedules, but they aren't self-disciplined. The activity becomes the deciding factor for them. They don't evaluate whether they should do something; they just say yes to everything. They do a lot but accomplish few long-range goals because they're involved in too many things.

Making Time

A third time usage technique is *making time*. Charles Buston observed, "If you want time, you must *make* it." Self-disciplined people control their time and routines rather than being controlled by them. They make time by planning carefully. Time makers don't mindlessly fill time slots; they thoughtfully decide how to spend spare minutes and hours. They don't overextend; they weigh opportunities and plan how to invest their time to get the best and greatest return.

Developing self-discipline takes time and energy, but it is well worth the effort. As we exert control over our lives and time through a succession of experiences, we eventually achieve an equilibrium and rhythm within ourselves that leads to successful life management. H. A. Ironside exhorts, "May we have grace to hold our spirits in godly subjection, that thus we become not like a city exposed to the ready assaults of its enemies."[3]

WORKSHOP

How much of a perfectionist are you? Rate yourself from 1 to 10, 10 being highest on the perfectionistic scale. That means if a statement is absolutely true, you would give yourself a 10. If it is usually true, depending on how often, you would rate a 7, 8 or 9. If it sometimes pertains to you, you'd score a 5 or 6. If it seldom applies, you'd give yourself a 2 or 3, and if it doesn't apply at all, you'd give yourself a 1. When you finish, tally your score, then read the category that describes you.

1. I believe making mistakes is the same as failing.
2. I preconceive outcomes and am upset if things do not turn out the way I think they should.
3. I am task-oriented.
4. I want things done my way or not at all.
5. I view things in terms of right or wrong, black or white.
6. I have difficulty making allowances for other people's shortcomings.
7. I would rather not try than risk failure.
8. I am meticulous.
9. I show my emotions.
10. I am very competitive.
11. I am logical.
12. I am self-willed.
13. I place unrealistic demands on myself.
14. I hold exaggerated expectations for others.
15. I am afraid to take risks and try new things.

If your score was in the 15 to 30 range, you're too laid back. You need to cultivate some concern and caring about what's happening in your life.

If your score was in the 31 to 70 range, you have a well-balanced, realistic approach to life. You use common sense and are able to live and let live.

If your score was in the 71 to 110 range, you are an extremely controlled person. You have definite opinions and set ways of doing things and sometimes expect the world to conform to your standards. You need to relax a bit and learn how to live and let live.

If your score was in the 111 to 150 range, you are a self-defeating perfectionist. You need to stop being so rigid and so hard on yourself and others. Step back and take a look at what's truly important in life.

Chapter Five   DISCIPLINING
                                        YOUR
                                    THOUGHTS

"We have the mind of Christ" (1 Corinthians 2:16).

I once heard a story about a man on trial for burglary. Although there was a great deal of circumstantial evidence against him and no witnesses to confirm that he had been home when the crime occurred, he adamantly professed his innocence until the final day of the trial. Much to everyone's surprise, he then changed his plea to guilty.

The judge was quite disgruntled. "Why didn't you enter a guilty plea before the trial started and save us all a lot of time and the taxpayers a hefty sum of money?"

The defendant hung his head. "I thought I was innocent, Your Honor, until I heard all of the evidence against me and now I know I'm not."

That humorous story points out a major biblical truth: We *are* what we think. (See Prov. 23:7.) What we think affects our mental and physical health, our aspirations and achievements, our speech, emotions, self-images, and the way we approach life and handle our circumstances. Our thoughts set up a kind of chain reaction that determines how we live and the sort of people we become. Frank Outlaw observed, "Watch your thoughts, they become words; watch your words, they become actions; watch your actions, they become habits; watch your habits, they become character; watch your character, for it becomes your destiny."[1]

Put this book aside for a moment and think about yourself—your opinions and attitudes and how you feel about yourself. Those thoughts determine your character, personality, and behavior. They determine what you like and dislike, accept and reject as true and important. Life and character, ultimately, are built on thought. Considering the monumental, formulative impact thoughts have on every phase of your life, imagine what would happen if you could learn to think like Christ!

One of the most astonishing statements the apostle Paul ever made was to the Corinthian Christians: "We have the mind of Christ" (1 Cor. 2:16). As Christians, we have within us the potential to think like Jesus thought, feel as He felt, reason as He reasoned, and respond as He responded. This lifts us above any human limitation toward wholeness and holiness of mind. Christ's presence brings stability and clarity to our thought lives. Isaiah observed, "The steadfast of mind Thou wilt keep in perfect peace, because he trusts in Thee" (Isa. 26:3).

Many times, instead of letting the Lord direct our thought processes, we try to tell Him how He should think and what He should do. We advise Him in our prayers how He should answer. When we impose our ideas on Him, we limit His influence in our lives and reduce our capacity for creative, righteous thinking.

In Isaiah 55:8–9, the Lord declared, "For my thoughts are not your thoughts, neither are your ways my ways . . . for as the heavens are higher than the earth, so are my ways higher than your ways, and my thoughts than your thoughts." There is no ground for comparison between the thoughts of even the most brilliant human mind and those of the Almighty. God's intellect, creativity, knowledge, understanding, wisdom, and resourcefulness far exceed ours. There is no limit to what could happen to our thought processes if we gave God full reign over them and claimed the mind of Christ.

There is absolutely no way to manage our lives and time satisfactorily without claiming the mind of Christ and disciplining our thoughts. Dr. Curtis Mitchell, in his book

Let's Live, states: "Not only does the Bible state that thought life is crucial; it also insists that the thought life is the source of our actions. What you say with your mouth, what you do with your hands, where you go with your feet really begins between your ears. These things are simply a reflection of what is going on in your mind. So, if the Bible is right, you can never control what you do and what you say until you begin to discipline your thoughts."[2]

RENEW OUR MINDS

If we can discover how to claim the mind of Christ *that is already ours by nature of our union with Him,* we will be equipped to manage our thoughts and emotions in ways that are pleasing to the Lord and satisfying to us. Scripture offers specific guidance to help us claim the mind of Christ. The first injunction is to "be renewed in the spirit of your mind" (Eph. 4:23). In that verse, renew means to make young and fresh. Spirit refers to our feelings, opinions, and attitudes. Renewing the spirit of our mind involves revitalizing thoughts, rejuvenating attitudes, and freshening up our feelings. We do that by controlling input.

Controlling Input

Each of us has a lifetime accumulation of impressions, facts, reactions, emotions, and attitudes stored in his brain's memory bank. God designed the human body so the mind operates through the brain. The mind has no more control over what goes into it than the stomach over what foods are put into it. Both organs absorb, digest, use, and expel whatever they are fed.

Renewing the spirit of our minds involves putting healthy, godly thoughts into our brains. You've probably heard the expression, "food for thought". Do we feed our minds junk food, or a healthy diet of fresh, stimulating, uplifting ideas? Empty and useless mental calories are as harmful to the well-being of our souls as junk food is to our bodies. Sugar, fat, caffeine, alcohol, salt, cholesterol—the list is endless—produce harmful physical effects. Worthless, unrighteous thoughts debilitate us mentally. We need to be aware of how various stimuli, such as the books and magazines we read and the television programs we watch, form and affect our thoughts just as we must be aware of how the foods, medications, and chemicals we consume affect our bodies.

If we're going to renew the spirit of our minds, we need constant, constructive input to counter all of the negative, debilitating, erroneous data that have accumulated in our brains and influence our actions and attitudes. Paul advised, "Set your mind on the things above, not on the things that are on earth" (Col. 3:2). James Allen observed, "A noble and godlike character is not a thing of favor or chance but is the natural result of continued effort in right thinking, the effect of long-cherished association with godlike thoughts."[3]

Developing a Different Mindset

Mind renewal involves developing a new and different mindset. Most of us pour concrete around our ideas and opinions. We set our minds: We say what we believe and act accordingly, shutting out any other possibilities. But we all know that the only thing that grows in cement is weeds. Beautiful foliage needs rich, fertile soil. Our minds should be like soil that can be enriched, tilled, and seeded with new ideas and watered and reshaped with truth and wisdom. James Allen noted, "A man's mind may be likened to a garden which may be intelligently cultivated or allowed to run wild; but whether cultivated or neglected, it must, and will, *bring forth*. If no useful seeds are put into it, then an abundance of useless weed seeds will fall therein, and will continue to produce their king."[4]

It's a fact of life that we reap what we sow. The only way to produce roses is to plant roses: We don't plant cactus and expect a lilac bush to sprout. The ideas we assimilate or *plant* in our brains grow into thoughts, feelings, and actions. We can't claim the mind of Christ without altering what we put into our heads.

Here in southern California, dichondra is one of the most popular varieties of lawn grass, which has a luscious, deep green color and small, circular leaves. It grows so close to the ground it doesn't need to be cut more than once a month, even during the peak growing season. Its arch enemy is a prolific weed called oxalis, which closely resembles dichondra except it has stickers and produces little yellow flowers when it seeds.

Last June, oxalis invaded our beautiful dichondra lawn. I dug for hours, pulling out leaves and roots, which wound like tentacles through the grass. I applied weed killer and checked daily for a reoccurrence. By the end of the summer, I was positive I had won the battle.

I was wrong! As soon as the weather warmed this March, the yard was a mass of oxalis almost overnight. It outnumbered the dichondra by about four to one. I'm afraid I'll never get rid of it now.

Ungodly, worldly thoughts are like that weed. Try as we might to control them, they keep cropping up unexpectedly once they take seed in our minds. It's best not to let them enter in the first place. We need to monitor input carefully because what goes in *will* come out. "Men imagine that thought can be kept secret, but it cannot; it rapidly crystallizes into habit."[5] Jesus warned, "Whatever is in the heart overflows into speech" (Luke 6:45 LB). Once something is programed into our thinking, it's difficult, if not impossible, to get rid of or maintain control over it.

Healthy Sources of Input

We receive input from many sources: literature, conversation, the media, and our own imaginations. Very little mind-renewing, positive, inspiring data comes to us through

television, radio, or films. Quality improves somewhat
when we talk with people, especially when we engage in
loving, edifying conversations. But the best input comes
through prayer, high quality literature, and the Scriptures.

Right reading is one of the best ways to renew our minds.
Reading the Word of God reveals the mind of the Lord to us.
It plants Christ's thoughts in our hearts and helps us develop
a godly mindset.

Good literature gives us pleasure and perspective; it
literally *freshens* our stale, sin-tainted thoughts. In "The Art
of Reading," Wilfred Peterson surmised: "Through books
you can encompass in your imagination the full sweep of
world history. You can watch the rise and fall of civiliza-
tions, the ebb and flow of mighty battles and the changing
pattern of life through the ages. Through books you can
orient your life in the world you live in, for books link the
past, the present and the future. Through books you can
know the majesty of great poetry, the wisdom of the
philosophers, the findings of the scientists. You can enrich
your spirit with the Psalms, the Beatitudes, the thirteenth
chapter of First Corinthians and all the other noble writings
that are touched with divine fire."[6]

When you read, remember you're reading to renew the
spirit of your mind, not merely to acquire information. Paul
cautioned that knowledge just for the sake of knowledge
makes people arrogant. (See 1 Cor. 8:1–2.) Our attitude
toward reading is as important as what we read. Thomas à
Kempis advised: "We should search the Scriptures for what
is profitable for our souls and not for beauties of language.
We ought to read devout and simple books as willingly as
those that are high and profound. If you wish to derive
profit, read with humility, with simplicity, and with faith;
and seek not at any time the fame of being learned."[7]

CAPTURING OUR THOUGHTS

Renewing our minds through positive input is an important part of thought discipline; so is *capturing our thoughts*. Paul urged the Corinthian Christians to "take captive every thought to make it obedient to Christ" (2 Cor. 10:5 NIV). We must entrap and capture our thoughts. If we do not, they can run wild.

Hostage situations quite often occur in this huge megalopolis, Los Angeles. When that happens, the S.W.A.T. team is called into action. Frequently, the police use a specially trained psychologist to negotiate and reason with the attacker. Last week the S.W.A.T. team dramatically rescued a woman and her three children from a disgruntled boyfriend who had held them hostage for eight hours.

The commander explained the strategy his men used to a newscaster: Before the police can capture a perpetrator and safely secure the release of prisoners, they first have to assess the situation, deciding exactly what's going on in the physical setting and in the mind of the assailant. Next, they have to plan a detailed strategy, outlining specifically what they will do. Finally, they must do whatever is necessary to free the hostages and capture the criminal.

The commander stressed that the police want to make certain that they are in control of the situation at all times. He said that the team takes note of the slightest movement or noise, explaining that sometimes a simple, seemingly innocent detail can make the difference between life and death. By using an expert in crisis intervention, "We try to break down the attacker's resistance and mess with his mind. If we can change his thinking, usually we achieve a satisfactory solution." Their ultimate goal, he concluded, is for the assailant to release the hostages and surrender peacefully.

The process for capturing our thoughts is similar to the one he described. First, we need to assess what we're thinking and decide exactly what's going on in our heads, instead of letting our minds aimlessly absorb whatever comes along.

Next, we need to develop a specific strategy for making our thoughts obedient to Christ. Dr. Earl Radmacher said, "Every thought is an occasion for control." We need to take careful note of *each* thought, even those that seem innocent or irrelevant because as they accumulate, they affect the overall pattern of our lives.

Finally, we should surrender our minds to Christ and ask Him to erase unsatisfactory, harmful, sinful thoughts. The Lord's abiding presence in our lives enables us to capture our thoughts rather than being held hostage by them.

TRANSFORM OUR THINKING

Another step in disciplining thoughts and claiming the mind of Christ is to *transform our thinking*. The formula for thought transformation is found in Romans 12:2, "Do not be conformed to this world, but be transformed by the renewing of your mind." The word "transformed" comes from the Greek word "metamorphose," which means to make a complete change from one form to another. Webster defines it as a striking alteration in appearance, character or circumstances. W. E. Vine calls it "the adjustment of the moral and spiritual vision and thinking to the mind of God, which is designed to have a transforming effect upon the life."[8]

The Larva Stage

Thought transformation doesn't occur immediately or instantaneously. Metamorphosis is a process that happens in stages. It is vividly illustrated in nature as a caterpillar changes into a butterfly. The first stage in that change is the *larva,* the form that hatches from the egg. During the first few hours of hatching, the outer skin of the caterpillar dries and hardens. When its covering becomes too confining and doesn't fit, the caterpillar sloughs it.

The larva stage of thought metamorphosis can be compared to the times we shed the hardened skin of preconceived ideas. We examine our opinions and shed those that confine the Spirit's movement in our lives. We slough the thought patterns that constrict our righteousness or personal growth and conform us to the world.

The Pupa Stage

The second stage of metamorphosis is the *pupa*. During this phase, the caterpillar stops moving and feeding. It spins a cocoon around itself and devotes all of its energy to changing into the adult form. The apostle Paul said, "When I was a child, I used to speak as a child, think as a child, reason as a child; when I became a man, I did away with childish things" (1 Cor. 13:11). The pupa period in thought metamorphosis represents our concentrated efforts to leave immature and willful reasoning and speculation behind, as we conscientiously work to become spiritually mature, discriminating thinkers.

The Adult Stage

The third stage in metamorphosis is the *adult*, when a beautiful butterfly breaks out of the cocoon, unfolds its wings, and flies into the world. For us, this reflects the times when we claim the mind of Christ. We consciously break away from old thought patterns, "put on the new self who is being renewed . . . according to the image of the One who created [us]," and walk, transformed, in the Spirit and newness of life (Col. 3:10).

The opposite of transformed thinking is thinking conformed to worldly ideas and opinions. There is no doubt that the world's value system affects our thinking. In her article "The Battle for the Mind," Jessie Penn Lewis stressed, "Because of the dangers of today, we cannot trust anything that comes from without. . . . Supposing a thought comes; it should be turned over and over and pondered in the presence of God."[9]

MEDICATE YOUR THOUGHTS

Thought metamorphosis is by nature an ongoing, never-ending process. Our minds are constantly being bombarded by the world, the flesh, and the Devil. Conversion is only the beginning of newness of life, and "a change of mind at conversion does not go deep enough to deliver the soul from the power of the enemy in your thought life and mental activities. The believer needs to recognize that the attacks of the emissaries of Satan are *primarily directed at the mind*. There is no part of the renewed believer which does not require guarding. This is especially true of the mind."[10]

We hear a lot in our society about mental illness. The disease of sin has warped people's minds. Before we can claim the mind of Christ, we need to acknowledge that portions of our thoughts *are* diseased. Then, we can medicate them with the healing balm of God's truth. Alexander Pope observed, "To know ourselves diseased is half the cure."

Sin-sick thoughts require diagnosis and treatment. Altering afflicted thought patterns will be tedious and painful. Self-examination is never easy. We don't like to admit that some of our thoughts are sick.

I recently read an article about a problem we've all heard about time and again. Some people ignore the symptoms of cancer, refusing to seek medical advice, because they are afraid of what the diagnosis will be. The author of the article stressed that these people in many cases are signing their own death warrants. They harm themselves because they don't want to face the truth. The article emphasized that denying the existence of the illness doesn't make it go away; rather, early diagnosis and treatment generally mean a cure.

The same is true with our minds. Dr. Curtis Mitchell believes that "mental hygiene is one of the great neglected areas of evangelical Christian circles."[11] Christians don't like to admit that their mental processes are diseased by sin because theoretically, they shouldn't be. So, they ignore the symptoms, delay diagnosis, and wait to act until their minds require prolonged treatment or major surgery, instead of a dab of spiritual antiseptic and a Band-Aid.

Denying unrighteous thoughts or trying to excuse them doesn't make them disappear. Untreated, they fester until they metastasize into permanent, disabling thought patterns. We cannot successfully manage our thoughts until we admit they are diseased and do something to bring about a cure.

RX FOR HEALTHY THOUGHTS

The Word of God contains a prescription for sick thoughts. The first step in the treatment is to *dwell on God and meditate on His Word*. One fact of which we can always be certain is that focusing our thoughts on Christ and the precepts of Scripture soothes and heals our minds, eliminating confusion and frustration. When we're upset or worried about something, dwelling on the problem only makes it seem worse. Meditating on the living and written Word— letting Christ occupy our minds—calms us and brings perspective. Thomas à Kempis, who devoted many years to pondering the Lord's truth and character, counseled, "Seek a convenient time to retire unto yourself and think often on the benefits of God."[12] It's difficult to think about Jesus and ponder sinful thoughts at the same time. The former negates the latter.

Dwell on Affirmatives

The second step in medicating sick thoughts is to *dwell on affirmatives*. Too often, we allow our thoughts to be overpowered by negatives to the extent that everything we do is affected. Edward E. Ford noted that "negative thoughts cause negative feelings; and negative feelings almost always result in negative behavior."[13] In Philippians 4:8, Paul exhorted the saints in Philippi to let their minds dwell on whatever is true, honorable, right, pure, lovely, of good repute, excellent, and worthy of praise. Dwelling on affirmatives rather than negatives uplifts and edifies our thought processes.

In "A Prayer for Enlightenment," Thomas à Kempis petitioned, "Lift up my mind, oppressed with the load of sins, and raise my whole desire toward heavenly things." Dwelling on positives, such as Paul suggested, lifts us toward heavenly things and medicates our thoughts with the healing power of righteousness.

Let Go of the Past

The third step in medicating sick thoughts is to *concentrate on the present*. It's all you have. Yesterday is gone, and tomorrow may never come. Gerhardt Tersteegen cautioned, "Do not think ahead and do not look back! Both bring unrest and are harmful. . . . The present moment must be your dwelling place. There only can we find God and His will."[14]

Many people debilitate themselves mentally by nurturing anger, bitterness, and hatred as they contemplate previous wrongs done to them. Dwelling on the past is futile: There is no way to change what has already happened. The only way to get beyond past hurts and clear them from your mind is to face them, accept them, and then leave them. Accept that all of the hurtful, negative circumstances of the past are a permanent part of you. You cannot erase or undo them. You may not even be able to understand them. But you can admit, and perhaps eventually accept and appreciate, that they occurred and that their influence in your life is a portion of God's gift of life. Your past *is* a part of you. Denying what has happened or how you feel about it won't change it.

You can't bury the past, but, propelled by God's grace, you can move beyond it.

Someone once said the greatest peace we can ever know comes from the art of letting go. Once we admit and accept the reality of the past, we must release it. *Let it go!* Replaying misfortunes in our mind and clinging to their pain is unhealthy. Instead, we should concentrate on the present. We must think positively and take affirmative action to control present events.

Getting beyond the negatives of the past isn't easy, but it is possible. Remember, we create our past by how we live in the present and approach the future. Writer Isabel Moore said, "Life is a one-way street. No matter how many detours you take, none of them leads back. Once you know and accept that, life becomes much simpler. Because then you know you must do the best you can with what you have and what you are and what you have become."[15] Even the most horrendous memories can be healed by dwelling on affirmatives and appreciating that "one-way street" God has prepared for you to travel.

Exercise the Mind

The fourth step in medicating and treating unhealthy thoughts is to *exercise our minds*. Mental calisthenics are as necessary to our well-being as physical exercises are to our bodies. The latest scientific studies show that, excluding physical impairment, the ability to think and learn does not deteriorate because of aging but from lack of use. As people get older, they stop exercising their minds and end up suffering from mental atrophy. The brain is a physical organ. Like the heart or lungs, it needs to be nourished and exercised regularly.

Maude Parker, in the poem "Legacy," exhorted, "Stretch your mind, as even you stretch your arms upward to the sky, lest numbness should set in. . . . Give it a daily task beyond its present strength and store it each day with treasure." Stretching our minds tightens mental flab and helps reshape our thoughts. We build mental stamina when we exercise our minds.

LET THE WORD OF CHRIST DWELL WITHIN YOU

Disciplining our thoughts means being ever sensitive to what Jesus would expect us to think, say, or do at any given moment. It means saturating our lives with the reality of His presence, surrendering our minds to Him moment-by-moment, letting "the Word of Christ richly dwell within [us]" (Col. 3:16), so His thoughts permeate our thoughts, His feelings our feelings and His actions our actions. Saint Patrick described what we can experience when we truly claim the mind of Christ in "The Shield of Faith":

> Christ be with me, Christ within me, Christ behind me, Christ before me, Christ beside me, Christ to win me, Christ to comfort and restore me; Christ beneath me, Christ above me, Christ in quiet, Christ in danger, Christ in hearts of all that love me, Christ in mouth and friend and stranger.

WORKSHOP

Listed below are some common negative thoughts each of us has from time to time. Maybe some of these are a consuming type of habit in your life. This workshop will help you claim the mind of Christ by replacing negative thoughts with positive Scripture excerpts. Read over the list. Then check ten of the thoughts most bothersome to you. Look up the Scripture and write, in your own words, how you can use each verse to claim the mind of Christ and overpower each negative thought. *Memorize the Scripture.* From now on, when you think that negative thought, remove it and claim the mind of Christ by quoting the Scripture and acting accordingly.

Negative Thought	Positive Scripture
1. Anger	Psalm 37:8
2. Anxiety	Philippians 4:6–7
3. Bitterness	Ephesians 4:30–32
4. Confusion	1 Corinthians 14:33
5. Disappointment	Matthew 11:28
6. Doubt	Matthew 21:21–22
7. Envy	Colossians 3:2
8. Fear	Psalm 34:4
9. Fretting	Philippians 2:14
10. Frustration	Proverbs 16:3
11. Futility	1 Peter 5:10
12. Guilt	Psalm 103:8–14
13. Grudge holding	Matthew 6:14–15
14. Hopelessness	Psalm 38:15
15. Irritability	Colossians 3:15–17
16. Impatience	James 1:2–4
17. Jealousy	1 Corinthians 13:4
18. Passivity	1 Corinthians 15:58
19. Pridefulness	Proverbs 8:13, 16:5
20. Resentfulness	Romans 12:19

Negative Thought	Positive Scripture
21. Selfishness	Romans 15:1–3
22. Self-pity	Romans 8:1
23. Sorrow	Matthew 5:4
24. Stubbornness	Proverbs 29:1
25. Vacillation	Joshua 24:15

Chapter Six

GIRDING YOUR MIND FOR ACTION

"Gird your minds for action" (1 Peter 1:13).

My son Brian is an avid sports fan. He enjoys watching almost every kind of athletic event on television. The other evening as I flopped onto the sofa after putting dinner in the oven, he was watching weight lifting. I've always been amazed that any human being can lift several times his weight without destroying his body. I know what happens to my back and arms when I pick up a grocery sack that's too heavy. Of course, professional weight lifters train vigorously, but they also wear a wide leather belt around their midsection to minimize the strain on their muscles and vital organs. They gird themselves so they can make the most of their strength and perform to the limits of their capabilities.

In some ways, Christianity is like weight lifting. If we're going to manage our thoughts and claim the mind of Christ, we need to follow the apostle Peter's advice to *gird our minds for action,* so we can make the most of our God-given strength and perform to the limit of our capabilities.

The word "gird" isn't common in today's society. It means to bind, fasten firmly, or encircle by surrounding an object with any flexible substance. In biblical times, soldiers girded themselves for battle by binding their swords around their loins.

Peter directs us to gird our minds. They must be firmly fastened to the way of Christ, not fashioned according to the world's philosophies. They must be in obedience to Christ.

Then, we will be prepared to battle whatever evil forces invade our souls or attack our righteousness.

I wish I could offer a simple, easy-to-follow formula for girding minds and managing thoughts, but I cannot. As I've struggled with this problem, I've realized there are no simple solutions. There are, however, certain attitudes necessary to control our thoughts in a Christlike way and attributes that follow when our thoughts are controlled and submitted to Christ.

It takes courage, desire, determination, humor, optimism and responsibility (I'll discuss responsibility in the next chapter) to control our thoughts. What follows is creativity, original thinking, integrity, and power. Blending all of these vital ingredients will gird our minds for action.

COURAGE

Girding our minds for action takes courage. We have to be willing to risk a new way of thinking. We have to unearth sinful thought patterns by examining them in the light of God's Word, then do something about them. Admitting, even to ourselves, that our thoughts are tainted, that we are wrong, that our fantasies are less than pure, our plans divisive, or our opinions unjust takes courage.

So does standing up for our convictions and doing what is right. Despite its restraints, the status quo is comfortable. It's easier to go along with the crowd than risk ridicule or rejection by choosing to march to a different drummer. But Christianity makes us different. Thinking like Christ means we won't think like most people.

Courage is rooted and grounded in God. Moses challenged the Israelites to "be strong and courageous." Then he counseled, "do not be afraid or tremble . . . for the Lord your God is the one who goes with you. He will not fail you or forsake you" (Deut. 31:6). The Lord supplies the courage to make us think differently. We have to be willing to apply it.

DESIRE

Desire is another aspect of girding up our minds and preparing them for action. We have to want to control and change our thinking. If we don't, we won't. A woman I know is drastically overweight. She is five-foot-four and weighs two hundred and eighty pounds. She makes no pretense about trying to lose weight. Recently, her doctor warned her that her blood pressure was dangerously high and insisted she go on a strict, sodium-free diet. She told him she would take the medicine he'd prescribed, but she wouldn't stop eating. I asked her why she won't follow her doctor's orders when her health is at stake. She replied, "Because I don't want to, and nobody is going to force me."

The same holds true for managing thoughts. If we don't want to order our minds, no amount of persuasion can force us, but eventually we'll suffer the consequences.

Most people are not self-motivated; they have to be stirred into action. But it takes self-motivation to discipline your thinking. For example, Betty had a habit of embellishing the truth. She always s-t-r-e-t-c-h-e-d the facts to make them more interesting. She actually invented lies in her mind to incorporate into her conversation. Her exaggerations weren't malicious or hurtful, just untrue.

When we studied the topic of "Truth vs. Lies" in our Bible study, the Spirit convicted her. She told me that she realized her thoughts were constantly infiltrated with lies. "I automatically exaggerate," she confessed.

She asked me if other people were aware she exaggerated, and I told her yes. The embarrassment she felt when she discovered she'd been so transparent motivated her to stop lying. She quickly found some good reasons why she should change her thought patterns: She badly wanted to build trust between herself and her friends; she wanted to obey the Lord by being truthful; and she wanted to relieve herself of the tremendous burden of trying to remember all of the inconsequential falsehoods she'd told, and to whom.

It was months before thinking truthfully came as readily to her as thinking dishonestly. In the process of changing, she realized the reason she lied was to make herself feel important. She had a poor self-image. She told me her next mind-renewal project would be learning to think more positively about herself. I'm sure she will because now she's motivated.

If you aren't self-motivated, ask the Lord to nudge you into action, to turn on your "wanter." Think of as many reasons as you can why you should improve your thought life. Make a mental list of all the benefits and blessings. Act enthusiastic, even if you aren't. Above all, decide on *one* specific change you want to make and work at it with all your might. Focus your attention on improving one thing, replacing one thought pattern, girding up one area at a time.

DETERMINATION

Determination closely follows desire as a must in thought management. Disciplining thoughts takes persistence and fortitude. Once you decide you want to control your thought life, you have to be willing to stick with it. You can't give up after the least little setback.

Abraham Lincoln is an example of what determination can do. He set his mind on becoming president of the United States. In 1831, he failed in business. In 1832, he was defeated for the legislature. In 1833, he again failed in business. In 1834, he was elected to the legislature. In 1835, his sweetheart died. As a result of that loss he suffered a nervous breakdown in 1836. In 1838, he was defeated for speaker; in 1840 for elector; in 1843, 1846 and 1848 for Congress; and in 1855 for the Senate. But he never gave up, although his defeats outnumbered his successes. Each defeat took him a step higher—from business to state politics, then to the national level. In 1860, he was elected president. Stick-to-it-tive-ness pays!

HUMOR

The next dynamic component in girding up our minds is humor. Samuel T. Coleridge noted that, "A mind is not completely well-organized that is deficient in a sense of humor." Thinking humorously can ease tense situations and relieve stress. I know a young woman who always flubbed job interviews because she was so nervous. One day, she took a tip from a friend and pretended that the interviewer was sitting behind the desk clad only in underwear. This private joke helped her relax and cleared her head.

Humorous thoughts can displace all sorts of negative emotions. It's difficult to stay angry when you're laughing. I was reminded of this the other evening as I watched an old movie on television. A husband and wife were having a fight, yelling at each other, and slinging verbal accusations and insults. The husband was so angry he mixed up his words, and the wife began to laugh. He took a sip of water to calm himself and spilled it down the front of his shirt. His wife laughed harder. Then, he started to laugh and promptly threw the rest of the water at her. They collapsed onto the floor laughing. The fight was forgotten; the anger dissipated. It was only a movie, but it was true to life. Humor can bring perspective to the most serious situations.

Humor has a healing power. Proverbs 17:22 states, "A joyful heart is good medicine." *Chicago Tribune* columnist Ronald Kotulak observed, "Jokes are no laughing matter to the brain. They are a type of release valve that enables us to think the unthinkable, accept the unacceptable, discover new relationships, adjust better and maintain our mental health. They are also funny. Without them we probably would be a dull, dim-witted society, trapped in a harsh world too serious to bear."[1]

Medical studies show that people who can laugh at themselves and look at the humorous side of their problems live longer and have fewer health problems. It's a proven fact that laughter has a tranquilizing effect: It improves the body's blood flow, decreases stressful messages that over-work our glands, and relaxes muscle tone.

Humor keeps us from taking life too seriously. Henry Ward Beecher said, "A man without mirth is like a wagon without springs . . . he is jolted disagreeably by every pebble in the road." Dr. S. I. McMillen, in his book *None of These Diseases,* states, "Our attitude of mind is a most important factor in determining whether we shall suffer from exposure to life's daily stress. . . . The sorrows and insults of daily living need not cause much trouble if we take them with the right mental attitude."[2] A right mental attitude includes perceiving and enjoying the humor in all kinds of situations.

OPTIMISM

Optimism is another necessity for girding our minds. Someone once said an optimist thinks this is the best of all possible worlds; a pessimist fears that's true. Optimists look on the bright side; pessimists have a negative mindset. Optimists view the glass as half-full; pessimists as half-empty. Optimists think about all of the good things that could happen; pessimists dwell on what catastrophes might occur. Optimists hope; pessimists worry. Optimists over-come circumstances; pessimists are overcome by them.

I once heard a story that is a perfect example of how pessimists think. When inventor Robert Fulton was giving his first public demonstration of his amazing steamboat, a pessimistic, it-can't-be-done man stood grumbling in the crowd. He kept repeating, "He can't start her. He can't start her."

When the boat belched a hearty bellow of steam and started moving, the startled man stared for a minute then started chanting, "Bet he can't stop her! Bet he can't stop her!"

Pessimism is one of the most difficult mental attitudes to

overcome because it is deeply ingrained in the pessimist's nature. Most people who are pessimistic learned it from adult role models when they were children; others became defeatists because they suffered too many blows in the school of hard knocks. Pessimism is a type of mental darkness that nurtures gloomy, negative, foreboding thoughts. As Christians we should be optimistic because we "are sons of light and sons of day. We are not of night nor of darkness" (1 Thess. 5:5).

Becoming an Optimist

But how can people change from being pessimistic to optimistic thinkers? First, they can stop placing their hope in the wrong things. Pessimists look at circumstances, which is enough to make anyone feel bad. They focus on what's happening rather than on what God is able to do. Two of their favorite phrases are "what if" and "yes, but."

If you're a pessimist, you need to plug your thoughts into God, who is the source of hope. The psalmist declared, "My hope is *in* Thee" (Ps. 39:7, emphasis mine). A Christian's hope isn't in education, politics, abilities, intellect, or material possessions but *in the Lord*. As the words of the magnificent hymn proclaim, "My hope is built on nothing less than Jesus' blood and righteousness. I dare not trust the sweetest frame, but wholly stand on Jesus' name."

Not only is our hope *in* God; it is *from* Him. David wrote, "My hope is *from* Him. He is my only rock and my salvation, my stronghold; I shall not be shaken" (Ps. 62:5–6). I suppose human beings on their own can conjure up some superficial form of hope, but it doesn't endure. It's only as strong as they are. But hope from God is "the hope of eternal life" (Titus 3:7).

How Bad Can It Be?

The second step in overcoming pessimism is to ask what's the worst that could happen. Contrive the most terrible, outlandish outcomes imaginable. Then, evaluate the odds of their happening. You'll soon realize how ridiculous most of your concerns are. Contrary to popular pessimistic belief, the worst usually doesn't happen.

I'd Rather Be Optimistic

Finally, to overcome pessimism, weigh the benefits of optimism. Paul said, "Hope does not disappoint" (Rom. 5:5). We should be "rejoicing in hope" (Rom. 12:12). The writer of Hebrews called it "an anchor of the soul, a hope both sure and steadfast" (Heb. 6:19). Optimistic thinking nurtures stability in our lives and anchors us to truth and reality. It is a source of happiness and a must for girding our minds.

CREATIVITY

Girding our minds for action stimulates creativity. One of the greatest and most misunderstood gifts God gave us is imagination, the ability to form mental images of things we can't perceive with our physical senses. It is part of our godlikeness since the Lord thought us up in His mind before He physically created us. (See Ps. 139:13–16.) Imagination is a magnificent blessing when properly managed. The Wright brothers dreamed of a machine that would fly. People thought they were crazy. If God had wanted man to fly, He'd have given him wings. Now a little more than seventy-five years later, we have probed the limits of outer space and can fly from coast to coast in about five hours.

Thomas Edison envisioned pictures that move and a lamp that would illuminate with a switch. As a result, we have the electric light, the phonograph, and motion pictures.

Renewing our minds involves using our imaginations to conceive new ideas and freshen up our thinking, as well as to devise innovative ways to handle problems, approach people, and live our Christianity in practical ways.

Daydreaming plays an important role in generating ideas and solving problems. We've been taught that daydreaming is a waste of time—I used to believe that—but properly applied, it can be an extremely constructive form of mental exercise. "The subconscious mind is the fireless cooker where our ideas simmer while we are [daydreaming]. Newton was loafing when he saw an apple fall and got the gravitation idea. While finding peace for his soul, Galileo watched the great swinging lamp. It gave him the idea of the pendulum swinging to and fro and a means of measuring the passage of time. Watt was relaxing in the kitchen when he saw steam lifting the top of the teakettle and conceived the idea of a steam engine. Many times we will get more and better ideas in two hours of creative loafing than in eight hours at a desk."[3]

What we commonly call daydreaming, Dr. Norman Vincent Peale refers to as "imaging" or "the forming of mental pictures." It is, he says, "a powerful and mysterious force in human nature that is capable of bringing about dramatic improvement in our lives. So powerful is the imaging effect on thought and performance that a long-held visualization of an objective or goal can become determinative." Imaging works best, he suggests, "when supported by a strong religious faith, and is reinforced by prayer."[4]

I recently interviewed members of the Lawrence Welk Musical Family for a cookbook I'm coauthoring with the wife of one of the performers. Almost without exception, they told me they had trained for and dreamed of pursuing musical careers from the time they were very young. Many talked about how the Lord had guided and directed them and brought those dreams to fruition. Without Christ's influence, our daydreams can quickly become immoral, foolish fantasies but under His tutelage, they can hone our insight and motivate us toward His will.

ORIGINAL THINKING

Creative thinking unleashes originality because each of us is different and unique. No two people are alike, so no two people think exactly the same. Girding our minds means learning to think for ourselves, then deciding what we believe and what is best for us as individuals. Unfortunately, many people don't think for themselves. They adhere to the philosophies, ideologies, and theologies that are presented to them by family, friends, associates, educators, or groups to which they belong. Then, they incorporate those ideas into their thought processes without evaluating content or issues. They operate on the mistaken notion that nonconformity is a form of defiance rather than an expression of individualism and that conformity is more acceptable and godly.

Conformity, in most cases, is overrated. It stifles creativity and suffocates self-expression. Overdone, it can be deadly. None of us will ever forget Jonestown. We wonder how such a thing could have happened. The answer is simple. Jim Jones demanded that his followers think as he thought, believe as he believed, and obey without questioning. The few who thought for themselves escaped; those who conformed perished.

One of my first realizations as an elementary school teacher was if I encouraged the children to be original thinkers, I could not impose too many restrictions. I never asked my students to walk in lines; I saw no purpose for it. I seldom had them raise their hands during discussions; I wanted them to be able to share ideas or answers as soon as the thoughts jelled in their minds, even if it meant two or three children were speaking at once. Usually, if they had to wait until I called on them, they lost the thought. I let them talk to one another when they were doing papers, as long as they stayed with the subject. My students were seldom quiet, but they were never rowdy or unruly, and they certainly learned how to think and express themselves.

God is creative. Possessing the mind of Christ means that magnificent attribute is available to us. Using our imaginations and developing original ideas, opinions, and ways of doing things help us become the men and women God designed us to be. He wants us to conform to the image of Christ, not to someone else's design.

INTEGRITY

A mind that is girded for action is also richly endowed with integrity. Integrity is the moral code each of us lives by—our beliefs concerning what is right and wrong, good and bad, holy and sinful. In "Age of Reason," Thomas Paine said, "It is necessary for the happiness of man that he be mentally faithful to himself." When we compromise our personal beliefs for any reason or let others impose their standards on us, we are being mentally unfaithful to ourselves. Taking the easy way out, going along with the crowd, giving anything or anyone control over our minds are all the same as giving others control over our lives.

Through the ages, great men and women of God have thought with integrity. Joshua determined that he would obey God. He carried out the Lord's orders to have the army march around Jericho, and an enemy was defeated. Ruth's thoughts were saturated with such unselfish love and loyalty that she would not compromise by letting Naomi return alone to Bethlehem. Shadrach, Meshach and Abednego would not compromise their faith in God, even under penalty of death. Their minds were so firmly set that they told King Nebuchadnezzar that even if God would *not* deliver them, "we are not going to serve your gods or worship the golden image that you have set up" (Dan. 3:18).

Daniel refused to sacrifice his beliefs about prayer, even though his life was threatened. Paul and many other of Christ's disciples boldly faced jeering crowds, hostile authorities, and imprisonment with no concern for their safety because they were mentally committed to spreading the Good News. David declared with confidence, "I *shall* walk in my integrity."

In his epistle, James referred to people who lack mental integrity as "double-minded." They think one thing one minute and something else the next. They do not know what they believe and don't stick to it if they do. Consequently, they are unstable in all their ways (James 1:8). Lack of mental integrity causes a lot of confusion in our lives. The old adage "To thine own self be true and it shall follow as the night the day thou canst be false to any man" is true. We must be mentally faithful to ourselves if we're going to gird our minds for action.

POWER

There is no denying the power of thought. Girding our minds harnesses that immense power. William James claimed, "Human beings can alter their lives by altering their attitudes of mind." We often wonder why certain people in similar circumstances, sometimes children from the same family, turn out so differently. Some are embittered by poverty and hardship; others turn to drugs or crime; and some literally rise above the situation and go on to do great things with their lives. I believe their success or failure is determined by their mental attitude.

My favorite magazine is *Reader's Digest*. My family teases me because when it arrives in the mail, I set aside that evening to read it. I amuse them by reading my favorite portions aloud. Each issue contains a "Drama in Real Life" story. These stories recount how ordinary people overcome immeasurable odds or stay alive in life-or-death situations. Almost without exception, the person's mindset plays a greater role in his survival than his physical know-how or dexterity.

The power of the mind is awesome. I visualize it as having

three components: will power, won't power, and Spirit power. Will power involves setting our minds to think in certain ways and to maintain particular thought patterns. Won't power works the opposite; it involves setting our minds not to think in certain ways, for example saying, "I will not allow these kinds of thoughts into my mind."

Psalm one records an example of both will power and won't power. The psalmist declares that he will not "walk in the counsel of the wicked, nor stand in the path of sinners, nor sit in the seat of scoffers." Rather, he will delight in God's law and meditate on it day and night.

Spirit power is, of course, the power of God within us. "God hath not given us the spirit of fear; but of *power* and of love and of a sound mind" (2 Tim. 1:7 KJV). The Holy Spirit of God actually acts as a supernatural power source that energizes our human spirits, so we can exert will power and won't power to develop sound minds. We cannot do this on our own. Only our omnipotent Lord can supply the kind of power that is necessary for thought management, but we must utilize it.

Power can be useful or harmful, depending on how it is used. When water is dammed and harnessed, it can generate electrical power but unleashed it can cause death and destruction. We are accountable for how we use the power of our minds.

WORKSHOP

I. This exercise will help you evaluate how well your mind is girded for action. Rate yourself on a scale of 1 to 10, 10 being best.

___ **1.** I think creatively and have an active imagination.

___ **2.** I want to control and change my thinking.

___ **3.** I have a good sense of humor.

___ **4.** I am mentally faithful to myself.

___ **5.** I am optimistic.

___ **6.** I do a good job of exerting will power and won't power.

___ **7.** I accept full responsibility for the words I speak, the actions I take, and the emotions I express.

___ **8.** I am aware of what I am thinking.

___ **9.** I am aware of what I am feeling.

___ **10.** I communicate my thoughts and feelings clearly and in acceptable ways.

If your score was 90–100, you're almost too good to be true.

A score of 60–80 indicates your mind is well girded, but you realize there's still room for improvement.

If your score was in the 30–60 range, you have some basic problems to overcome in the area of thought management.

A score of 10–20 indicates that you need to work diligently at changing your thought patterns and improving your mental attitude.

Chapter Seven

TAKING RESPONSIBILITY FOR YOUR THOUGHTS

"If we say we have no sin, we are deceiving ourselves" (1 John 1:8).

Courage, desire, or determination will not help us harness our thoughts unless we first believe we are the ones responsible for them. In his book *Caring Enough to Confront,* David W. Augsburger stresses, "The thoughts I think, the words I speak, the actions I take, the emotions I feel—they are mine, for them I am fully responsible."[1] It is *our* responsibility to change our behavior and attitudes toward life.

To avoid responsibility for our actions, we sometimes blame others, circumstances, our upbringing, our environment, society, our spouses, or even the Lord. A popular advice column recently carried a letter from a young married woman who, although by her own admission was married to a sweet, wonderful man, had fallen madly in love with her brother-in-law, also married.

"I try, but I can't stop thinking about him," she wrote. "He is always on my mind. When my husband and I make love, I pretend I'm with him. When I sleep, I dream about him. I think he might care for me, too. What should I do?"

The columnist told her to forget her brother-in-law and count her blessings. Good, though incomplete, advice. That young woman has a severe problem. She definitely needs to exert a huge dose of won't power and to accept responsibility for her thoughts, or she's going to hurt herself and a lot of innocent people.

ASSUME RESPONSIBILITY FOR YOUR THOUGHTS

The Bible can advise us how to assume responsibility for our thoughts. First, we consider their source: Are they coming from the world, the flesh, the Devil or the Lord? Paul warned the Christians in Colossae to "see to it that no one takes you captive through philosophy and empty deception, according to the tradition of men, according to the elementary principles of the world, rather than according to Christ." (Col. 2:8). Matthew Henry noted that when the admonition was written, "The Jews governed themselves by the traditions of their elders. The Gentiles mixed their maxims of philosophy with their Christian principles, and both alienated their minds from Christ.[2] Girding our minds means making sure that Christ is the source of our thoughts.

Destroy Speculations

Second, accepting responsibility for our thoughts means we should destroy speculations. The young woman who wrote that letter to the columnist was speculating, playing "mind games," about how her brother-in-law felt about her and what making love to him would be like. In her case, conjecture generated sexual fantasies. There is no end to the kinds of thoughts speculation can spawn. Speculation is dangerous because it isn't based in fact; rather, it woos us away from reality and righteousness.

Destroy Lofty Thoughts

Paul cautioned the Corinthian Christians to destroy "every lofty thing raised up against the knowledge of God" (2 Cor. 10:5). We must discard any ideas or opinions that disagree with God's truth and standards by examining whether our thoughts coincide or conflict with God's Word and His holiness.

Confess and Accept Cleansing

Third, accepting responsibility for our thoughts incorporates confession and cleansing. We are human, so we will have sinful, immoral thoughts. "If we say we have no sin, we are deceiving ourselves" (1 John 1:8). We can either brood on them and regurgitate them in some way or acknowledge their existence and turn them over to God. When we are willing to label specific thoughts as sins and admit to God that they are impure, "He is faithful and just to forgive us our sins, and to cleanse us from all unrighteousness" (1 John 1:9 KJV).

Confession prefaces cleansing. When we confess, God cleans our *dirty* minds. Confession is our responsibility; cleansing is the Lord's. After David had committed treason, murder, and adultery and was convicted of his sin by the words of the prophet Nathan, he pleaded with God for pardon. "I know my transgressions," he confessed, "and my sin is ever before me. Against Thee, Thee only, I have sinned, and done what is evil in thy sight" (Ps. 51:3–4).

Even though David confessed, he still felt dirty. He begged God to *wash* him from his iniquity, *cleanse* him from his sin, *purify* him. "Create in me a clean heart, O God," he pleaded, "and renew a steadfast spirit within me" (Ps. 51:10). Each of us is responsible to follow David's example: to confess our sinful thoughts and trust the Lord to cleanse them.

Express Thoughts

One final step in assuming responsibility for our thoughts is learning how to express them in acceptable, understandable ways. A curious thing about thoughts is that they generate feelings. When we show emotion, we are expressing our thoughts. Feelings are actually emotional reactions we have about what's happening in our minds. Behavior is the way we choose to express those feelings.

Sometimes, a person tries to deny or repress her emotions; however, that doesn't eradicate or change them. Eventually those thoughts will resurface. Choosing how and when to express them makes more sense than burying or ignoring them. Bottled-up thoughts and feelings can be corrosive and explosive. As acid corrodes metal, so do repressed emotions work on you internally, causing physical and emotional problems. Such a person reaches a point where she can no longer contain her feelings, and she spews them out, often at inappropriate times on innocent people.

Yet many people, including Christians, are afraid to express their thoughts and feelings. I believe this is because they have some serious misconceptions about emotions. One misconception is that women have different emotions than men. That is not true. Both men and women feel love, anger, guilt, joy, grief. People of both sexes experience the same emotions, but different people, regardless of their gender, express them differently.

Another common misconception is that the more mature we are, the less emotional we are. As we age, we hopefully learn how to handle and display our emotions, but they don't decrease. If anything, the intensity of our feelings increases through the years, as we recognize what is and isn't important and how precious life is.

Believing you have to understand *why* you feel as you do before you can change is also erroneous. If you're so angry that you feel like throwing things and screaming, channeling your emotions is more important than analyzing them, which may only intensify rather than explain them.

Another misconception about emotions is that we should express only positive ones. We need to express all kinds of emotions. It's the manner in which we display them that matters. We need to accept responsibility for finding suitable ways to vent negative emotions. "The goal is not to eradicate feelings for it is natural and healthy to experience many different emotions. Instead, we seek to enjoy our emotional nature rather than being in bondage to it."[3]

What Am I Thinking?

There are four steps involved in properly expressing thoughts. The first is being aware of what we're thinking at all times. Every waking moment the brain is programing and digesting ideas, information, and responses. We need to stay in touch with what's going on in our heads. To get in touch with our thoughts, we should pause for a few moments several times every day to reflect on what we're thinking and feeling. This is especially necessary when we're faced with conflict or need to make important decisions. We've all been cautioned to stop, take deep breaths, and count to ten when we're angry because pausing forces us to calm down and gain control over our thoughts and emotions. We don't need to do that only when we're upset. If we're going to manage our thoughts, we need to be continually aware of what's going on in our minds.

What Am I Feeling?

The second step in properly expressing thoughts is closely related to the first: Identify exactly what we are feeling. Surface reactions aren't necessarily honest expressions of what we're feeling. The other day as I was shopping, a young mother was frantically searching the store for her three-year-old son. Several of us joined in. Just as the chief security officer arrived and started questioning the woman, an impish little boy came sauntering out from behind a rack of pants, acting as if he hadn't a concern in the world. His mother rushed to him, sobbing and screaming his name and hugged him until he was breathless. Then in the midst of her tears, she started swatting his bottom and yelled, "I'm so mad at you I could kill you! Don't you *ever* do anything like that again!"

That mother wasn't angry; she was frightened and relieved. When children tell a parent, "I hate you," they're expressing frustration, resentment, anger—some deeper emotion they can't define. Such outbursts generally are symptoms of deeper, unidentified feelings rather than honest expressions of what is said.

One simple way to get in touch with your true feelings is to play the "adjective game." Name as many words as possible that you believe might describe how you feel. Ann shared that she did this when she found out that one of her closest friends had told a hideous lie about her to a mutual acquaintance. "I started with 'angry,' but that didn't begin to describe what I was feeling. Neither did 'hurt' or 'defensive.' It was much more than that," she said. "But when I said 'betrayed' and 'stupid,' I knew I had discovered the truth. I had been unquestioningly loyal to that woman for years and I felt she had betrayed me, but most of all I felt totally foolish for trusting her."

The advantage of identifying and admitting our feelings is that, once we do, we can decide what to do with them. We can neutralize them.

Neutralizing Thoughts and Feelings

Neutralizing is the third step in learning how to express thoughts properly. It is doing whatever is necessary to avoid reacting automatically or unseemly on whatever feelings we might be experiencing at any given moment. Neutralizing is backing off from an emotion until we loosen its unholy hold and decide how to handle it in an appropriate way. When a car is idling in neutral, the engine is running, but the vehicle doesn't move. It can't move until the driver decides where to go, slips it into gear, and accelerates. Neutralizing is slipping our thoughts and feelings into neutral until we decide where to go with them. This gives us breathing room and provides an opportunity for us to step aside and assess a situation.

For example, once Ann defined her feelings toward her friend who had lied about her, she calmed down. Then she realized she needed to find some way to talk to the woman about the problem. If she hadn't identified then neutralized her emotions, she'd have opted for an angry confrontation. Instead, she went to her friend and asked her to explain why she had lied about her. Eventually, their relationship was restored.

What Should I Do?

Planning a satisfactory way to respond and react is the final step in learning how to express thoughts. In his book *The Christian Use of Emotional Power,* H. Norman Wright lists several unacceptable, unhealthy ways people express their thoughts and feelings, such as taking out their feelings on others, blaming others, getting even, or verbally attacking someone. There are better ways.

Actually, one of the best ways to neutralize and rechannel unsatisfactory thoughts and emotions is to *act* in opposition to them. Controlling what we do is easier than controlling what we think or feel. No one can read our minds or see our thoughts, but we can't hide our actions. Consequently, *it's easier to act ourselves into a new way of thinking than to think ourselves into a new way of acting.*

In the book *Why Marriage?,* Edward E. Ford says, "The chain of events in everyday living goes like the following: think about what to do; make a judgment, then a plan, then do the plan or behavior. It is difficult to say which of these three functions comes first, but we can be sure that changing behavior will ultimately change our feelings. The feelings might not change right away, but eventually they will change as the behavior reinforces our thinking patterns and processes."[4]

We've already established that thoughts give birth to emotions and behavior, so what goes on in our minds affects everything we say and do. But actions can also greatly influence thought. For example, if you lose your temper easily, instead of blowing your stack, yelling at the kids, and kicking the dog, take a deep breath, speak softly, and act calmly. You'll find that the initial surge of anger will dissipate. Then you can decide if your anger is legitimate and how to express it in a suitable manner, instead of reacting to the first thoughts and feelings that pop into your mind.

Some people believe that acting contrary to a thought or emotion is being hypocritical, but it isn't. It's practicing self-control. H. Norman Wright noted, "While we usually are not able to control an emotional response to a particular stimulus, we CAN control how we express that emotion. If you feel hate, you do not have to act hateful."5

Solomon advised this technique in Proverbs 25:21–22. He said, "If your enemy is hungry, give him food to eat; and if he is thirsty, give him water to drink; for you will heap burning coals on his head, and the Lord will reward you." The implication in that text is that we are to act contrary to ungodly thoughts, regardless of what we're feeling. It *is* possible to act ourselves into a new way of thinking. We *can* change our thoughts and feelings by communicating them in acceptable ways.

HINTS FOR COMMUNICATING WHAT YOU'RE THINKING

If we are to assume responsibility for expressing our thoughts, we must determine what to say and when and how to say it. Here are some constructive communication techniques that may prove helpful.

Be specific. State exactly what you're thinking and feeling, then explain why. Tell your child, "I'm disappointed that you got a C in history because I know you're capable of doing better." Tell your spouse, "I'm angry because that's the fourteenth time I've stumbled over the shoes you left in the middle of the room. It upsets me that you won't walk to the closet and put them away."

Go to the source. Talk *to* the person(s) who have touched you, not *about* them. If you're frustrated with your boss, don't talk behind his back to another employee. If your wife prepares an outstanding meal, tell her. Don't wait to brag about her culinary talents to your friends when you're playing golf. Confront or compliment face-to-face.

When expressing negatives, *attack the problem, not the person.* Don't attach judgmental labels, like "you are." Instead, share your reaction to the situation: Speak in the first person. Say, "I think" or "I feel." For instance, if your best friend is always late, don't accuse her of being selfish and inconsiderate but say, "When you're late, I feel you aren't interested in doing things with me." When you disagree with someone, say, "I disagree."

Deal only with the case in point. This may be difficult if you've been compiling a mental list of grievances against someone or harboring ill will. If your neighbor's dog digs up your geraniums, yelling about the time his kids broke your window or the time he neglected to return your hammer for six months isn't going to solve the immediate problem of his renegade bulldog. Proverbs 25:8 cautions, "Do not go out hastily to argue your case." Digging up the past in the heat of the moment doesn't accomplish anything, except to block honest, intelligent communication. If there are other issues that need to be settled, find the right way, time, and place to handle them.

Make contact when you communicate. Impersonal communication creates a higher risk of misunderstanding. Gestures, like sitting knee-to-knee or standing toe-to-toe, looking another person directly in the eyes or touching someone on the arm, generate warmth and intimacy and break down hostility. Just yesterday, one of my friends told me she gets so upset with her twenty-seven-year-old daughter that she feels like spanking her. Instead, she gives her a big hug, then holds her hand when she offers criticism. Contact makes you aware that you're dealing with living, feeling people, not abstract thoughts and opinions. Consequently, you are more sensitive and caring.

Be willing to listen. Communication is a two-way street.

After you share your thoughts and feelings, you have to let the other person respond in kind, without interrupting or making value judgments. Listening is as much a part of communication as talking. If you want to know what's in someone's heart, you have to listen to his words.

Girding our minds for action is a vital part of life management. W. E. Vine explains that the word "gird" is taken from the circumstances of the Israelites as they ate the Passover meal in readiness for their journey. He states that girding the mind means "the Christian is to have his mental powers alert."[6] In preparing for the Exodus, every Hebrew family had to sacrifice a perfect lamb, apply its blood to the lentil and doorposts of their home, and eat the Passover meal, celebrating in advance their deliverance from death and their release from bondage. We prepare or gird up our minds for action by claiming the mind of Christ, saturating our thoughts with the redemptive power of His blood, and partaking of the feast of His Word. We are then released from bondage or unrighteous thought patterns to live victoriously in the Spirit.

WORKSHOP

I. The Bible uses many words to describe various kinds of thoughts. Look up each word in a dictionary and write its definition. Next, using a KJV, look up the corresponding Scripture verse and write it, substituting the dictionary definition in the place of the words "think" or "thought." The first one is done for you. *Nouns* = Types of thoughts

1. A word *something said or spoken*	Deuteronomy 15:9 *Beware, lest there is a base word*—something you will say or speak—*in your heart.*
2. A device	Proverbs 12:5
3. Doubts, opinions	Psalm 139:23
4. Will, desire	Psalm 139:17
5. Reflecting	Hebrews 4:12
6. Contrivance	2 Corinthians 10:5
7. Anxiety, worry	Matthew 6:25
8. Wish	Job 17:11

II. The Bible also uses many words to describe different ways of thinking. Look up the definition of each "thought" word in a dictionary and write its definition. Next, look up

the corresponding Scripture and write it, substituting the
dictionary definition in place of the word. *Verbs* = ways of
thinking

1. to esteem   Philippians 2:6

2. to reason   1 Corinthians 13:11

3. to understand   Ephesians 3:20

4. to consider   Matthew 5:17

5. to expect   James 1:7

6. to suppose   Matthew 16:15

7. to devise, design   Psalm 48:9

8. to remember   Nehemiah 5:19

Chapter Eight

GLORIFYING GOD IN YOUR BODY

"Do you not know that your body is a temple of the Holy Spirit who is in you, whom you have from God, and that you are not your own? For you have been bought with a price: therefore glorify God in your body" (1 Corinthians 6:19–20).

Jack LaLanne's life is entertaining and inspirational to many of us living in southern California. He was a proponent of physical fitness and health foods decades before the recent craze swept the country. When we moved to California in 1958, he already had opened a chain of health spas and had an exercise program on television. He celebrated his seventieth birthday by pulling a fleet of seventy boats behind him, each containing at least one person, as he swam a mile in Long Beach Harbor with his hands and feet bound together. After the feat, a reporter asked him what advice he could offer for staying in such good shape. He replied, "Take care of your body. It's the only one you'll have."

Life is a gift from God that comes wrapped in a package called the body. As a Christian, your body is very special. It is much more than a carcass that covers and protects your physical organs and shelters your soul. According to Scripture, your body is the temple of the Holy Spirit. It became a temple when Christ came to dwell in your heart through faith and the Spirit of the living God established permanent residency within you.

YOU, A TEMPLE

Now that we've analyzed the internal aspects of self-management, we need to take a look at the external. To clearly understand what being the dwelling place of almighty God means, we need to dig into the Old Testament to study the physical structure of the temple, so we can make some comparisons and draw some conclusions.

The first section of the temple, which surrounded the other buildings, was *the outer court* or *the yard*. The first thing we notice when we go to someone's house is their yard. As a matter of fact, we see many more yards than we do interiors.

When I go on my morning walk, I pass dozens of houses in my neighborhood, but I've only been in about ten of them. I don't know about you, but I make assumptions about the inside's appearance based on what I see on the outside. One house I pass has a totally unkempt lawn, which consists of crab grass, dandelions, and various other weeds. The paint on the house is peeling. Trash has blown into the yard and accumulated against the fence. The latch on the side gate is broken, as is a front window that's been taped over with cardboard for months. The mailbox is rusty, and there are usually three or four yellowed newspapers lying in the driveway. I have a definite picture in my mind of what the interior of that house must look like.

Fair or not, most people judge us by our outer courts: how we look and how well we maintain our bodies. We meet more people casually than in an intimate setting, so not many get *into* our lives. Consequently, the courtyard of our temple—the way we dress, talk, and conduct our business and lives—is extremely important. It's the first, and sometimes only, reflection others see of Jesus Christ. If it's sloppily kept, littered with the trash of worldliness, and infested with the weeds of sin, people will notice and judge us and our Lord accordingly.

A GATEWAY TO GOD

The next major edifice of the Old Testament temple was *the gate*. This entryway was more than just a door; it was a reflection of Christ, the coming Messiah. It was lavishly draped with beautiful cloth: some a heavenly blue, indicating that the Messiah would be sent by the Father from heaven; some purple, the color of royalty, denoting that He would be King of Kings and a Royal Priest; some scarlet, the color of the sacrificial blood, typifying the Christ as the coming Savior; and some silver, the color of purity, foretelling that Jesus the Messiah would be sinless and holy. Every Jew who passed through the temple gate was reminded of those truths about their promised Deliverer.

The gate to each of our temples is the gate of example. It should serve as a doorway to God, an opening through which others can enter into the presence of the Lord. Too often, our temple gate is an unwelcoming sight that would hardly woo anyone toward Christ. It's full of splinters, covered with dirty fingerprints, and has loose hinges due to lack of maintenance or neglect. Jesus Christ expects each of our temples to have a well-oiled, properly maintained gate, one that reflects Him in all His glory as the Son of God.

THE TABERNACLE

The temple gate led into *the tabernacle,* a building that in some ways resembled the sanctuaries in our modern churches. It had two rooms. The outer one contained the altar of burnt offering where the sacrifices for sin were made and a brass laver (washbowl) where priests bathed before ministering. The inner room consisted of two chambers, *the Holy Place* and *the Most Holy Place,* frequently referred to as the Holy of Holies. These compartments were separated by a veil made of the finest blue, purple, and scarlet linen. The Holy Place contained a table of shewbread, a candlestick, and an altar of incense. The Holy of Holies housed the ark of the covenant.

Each of these artifacts has a special significance in the temple or life of a Christian. The altar represents Christ's sacrifice on the cross and the presentation of our bodies to Him as living, holy sacrifices. (See Rom. 12:1.) In the tabernacle, the brass laver signified cleansing from sin. It was a *shadow* of our cleansing from sin by Christ's shed blood. Some theologians believe it symbolizes the sacrament of baptism. Others maintain it represents confession and a life that has been washed and cleansed with the blood of Christ.

The table of shewbread was a symbol of gratitude for God's daily provision to His people and is a reminder to us of the *daily bread* of love and blessings He lavishes on us. The candlestick reflects the light of God's Word that is buried in our hearts and delivers us from the darkness of sin. The incense, which was meant to be burned before kings, signifies Jesus' position as Lord in our lives and symbolizes a lifestyle that befits royalty. We *are* children of the King. Paul noted, "As far as God is concerned, there is a sweet, wholesome fragrance in our lives. It is the fragrance of Christ within us, an aroma to both the saved and the unsaved all around us" (2 Cor. 2:15 LB).

HOLY, HOLY, HOLY

The last place we come to in the tabernacle is the awesome *Holy of Holies* where God met with, spoke to, and dwelt among His people in all of His glory. (See Exod. 25:22.) It contained the ark of the covenant, which was totally symbolic of Christ. It was made of common acacia wood, signifying the humanity and humility of our Lord. It was overlaid with gold, attesting to His deity. Two angels (cherubim) graced the top of the ark. The angel of righteousness was positioned on the left. Sprinkling it with sacrificial blood restored fellowship between God and His people, just as we're reconciled with God by the blood the perfect, sacrificial Lamb shed on Calvary. The angel of justice was positioned on the right. Sprinkling it with blood satisfied God's sense of justice, just as Christ's death became a propitiation for our sin.

The ark contained three items: a copy of the Law, pointing out the sin of God's people and their need for a Savior; Aaron's rod that budded, a reminder that sin broke fellowship between God and man but that life would be restored through Christ's resurrection; and a pot of manna, illustrating that God always provides for His own and that He will "supply all our needs, according to His riches in glory through Christ Jesus" (Phil. 4:19).

A veil separated the Holy Place from the Most Holy Place. It was ripped from top to bottom at the moment Christ died, showing that His final sacrifice provided unlimited access into the presence of God from that moment on. Before Calvary, only a high priest could approach God in the Holy of Holies on the Day of Atonement. The rest of the people had access to Him only through their sacrificial rituals. But, "when Christ appeared as a High Priest of the good things to come, He entered . . . the holy place once for all, having obtained eternal redemption" (Heb. 9:11–12).

Can you imagine what going into the very place where God dwelt must have been like to a high priest; how standing in the very presence of God must have felt; how awestruck he must have been? What? *Do you not know that your body is a temple of the Holy Spirit who is in you?* (1 Cor. 6:19).

Grasp this truth! If you are a Christian, your body *is* the Holy of Holies where almighty God abides in all of His glory. *You* are a temple! You *are* a temple! You are a *temple!*

Those of us who are *in* Christ don't merely have the privilege of entering the Most Holy Place: We *are* a Holy of Holies. The God of the universe dwells within each of us.

A FIRM FOUNDATION

God lives in us only because of Christ, who is the foundation for our lives, the rock on which we build our faith. The temple had no constructed floor. This indicates that there is nothing we humans can do to qualify as a dwelling place for God or to make ourselves holy: "No man can lay a foundation other than the one which is laid, which is Jesus Christ. We have a building from God, a house not made with hands" (1 Cor. 3:11, 2 Cor. 5:1). God has laid the foundation of our temples. It's up to us to maintain the structure.

MAINTAINING YOUR TEMPLE

God doesn't take up residency in our lives because He needs a place to stay. He has a definite purpose for turning our bodies into temples. Paul stated that the Lord dwells within us so we can glorify God in our bodies. (See 1 Cor. 10:31.) W. E. Vine explains that glorifying God means "to magnify, extol, praise, ascribe honour to Him, acknowledging Him as to His being, attributes and acts."[1]

Glorifying God in our bodies requires more than taking care of the external, although "ground tending" is an important part of the process. I would encourage every one of you to read a good biology or physiology textbook. I'd also recommend the book *Intended For Pleasure* by Dr. Ed and Gaye Wheat, published by Fleming H. Revell, which includes a thorough, illustrated explanation of both the male and female reproductive systems.

But a general knowledge about the human body is not enough. Each of us needs to know how her own body functions. Most of us are so accustomed to living with ourselves that we don't think about our physiological makeup. For example, someone who always feels tired assumes that's normal and never suspects a hormone deficiency or anemia. A person who suffers from chronic sinus headaches learns to live with them, instead of exploring the cause and seeking a cure. Each of us is different. No two bodies function exactly the same. If we're going to glorify God in our bodies and properly tend our temples, we need to know as much about our God-created physical uniqueness as possible.

How many of you can answer the following questions? Are you a morning or night person? How much sleep do you need to get rested and stay healthy? Can you describe what your basic metabolism is like? Do you know why you fatigue easily or always have an abundance of energy? What health problems might you have inherited? What can you do to minimize the chances of its occurrence? If you're taking any kind of medication, exactly what is it supposed to do and what are its side effects? Does it react negatively with any other medication or foods? Do you have good posture? What is your resting heart rate? Your blood pressure? Do you suffer from any known allergies? What's your body type? What kind of eating program should *you* follow? What kind of exercise program would be best for you?

WHY BOTHER?

You may be asking, "Why bother?" especially if you're feeling fine and have no apparent physical problems. Part of life management is tending the temple, staying healthy, and being aware of what's happening in your body. Paul reminded the Corinthian Christians, "you have been bought with a price," the precious blood of Jesus (1 Cor. 6:20). You should do everything within your power to properly maintain your physical temple. When I die, I want it to be because God takes my life. I don't want to waste it through ignorance, oversight, or neglect.

People who take their bodies for granted are like a person who buys an expensive automobile but does nothing to maintain it. Car maintenance includes more than filling the gas tank, adding oil, and occasionally visiting a car wash. It also includes taking care of minor problems as soon as they arise to save major repairs later. The same is true of a person's body. Body maintenance is wiser and less costly, in terms of pain, as well as expense, than repairing a breakdown.

Let's look at some reasons why knowing about your body is important. Knowing whether you are morning or night persons is a clue to how your internal clock operates. It will help you decide when you perform best and are most productive. Each of you should know how much sleep you require. You think and perform better when your body is rested and your minds refreshed.

Your basic metabolism determines how quickly or slowly, efficiently or ineffectively your body processes food, how many calories your body requires, how your food is digested, how much fat your body absorbs, and your energy level.

For example, I know I need about six hours sleep every night, but about once every three or four months I'll be absolutely exhausted by 8 P.M. and need a full twelve hours. Then I "crash." I can maintain my weight on 1,100 calories a day and lose two pounds a week by reducing my intake to 900 calories. That knowledge helps me control my weight and balance my diet.

Knowing about inherited potential health problems can help prevent them. My family has a predisposition toward high cholesterol, so I watch my intake carefully. Our son Brian, who is adopted, has a history of diabetes in his background, so I try to limit his consumption of sugar and watch for symptoms.

Medication of any kind affects your body. Recent findings indicate that taking an aspirin every day thins the blood and reduces high blood pressure. Antibiotics made Brain hyperactive and kept him awake when he was young. I later found they contained caffeine. Over-the-counter allergy medicines cause drowsiness. Most eye drops that relieve redness and itching contain warnings on their labels cautioning people with glaucoma not to use them. Certain kinds of blood-pressure medicine can cause impotence in males. An acquaintance of mine took "water pills" to help her lose weight. She was rushed to the hospital with an apparent heart attack. As it turned out, the diuretic she was using had severely depleted her potassium level. Potassium is a mineral that helps control muscle function and heartbeat. She almost killed herself because she didn't know about the side effects of her "reducing" medicine.

Poor posture affects the entire body, from the way blood circulates to the way vital organs function. I remember how my fifth-grade teacher, Miss Esther Dean, used to tell the class: "Sit up straight. Throw those shoulders back. You can't get blood to your brain when your lungs are squashed."

Your resting heart rate is the number of times per minute your heart beats when you are inactive. It tells how hard your heart is working. The best time to measure it is in the morning before you get out of bed. Take it every morning for a week then average the rates. If it's high (85 beats per minute or over), you need to take steps to lower it—usually some kind of aerobic exercise will help. When I started doing aerobics six years ago, my resting heart rate was 79. Now it's 51. That means my heart is going to last longer because it's working half as hard.

Your heart beats about 100,000 times every twenty-four hours and pushes your blood through 60,000 to 100,000 miles of blood vessels. Blood pressure tells how well the blood is flowing and how much pressure it is exerting on the walls of the arteries. If the arteries are clogged or blood forms clots in them, the pressure is higher, indicating something must be done to decrease that stress. High blood pressure (hypertensive disease) has been called the silent killer because its symptoms usually go undetected until a stroke, coronary heart attack, angina pectoris, or other severe or fatal conditions occur. High blood pressure is not curable, but it is treatable and controllable when discovered in time. Keeping tabs on your blood pressure can prolong your life.

Generally speaking, allergies are more annoying than deadly, but they can affect the overall state of your physical and mental health. They cause all sorts of discomfort: from runny noses to sneezing fits, insomnia, depression, and excessive nervousness. My son Brian is so severely allergic to chocolate that it affects his moods. A few minutes after eating it, my easy-going, happy-go-lucky kid turns into a short-tempered grouch. It also gives him morning sickness for several days after he eats it. Since allergies detract from the quality of life, it's important to isolate and treat them, preferably by controlling diet and environment.

KNOWING YOUR BODY TYPE

Knowing your body type is important in life management; it can help you determine an appropriate exercise and eating program. Skeletal structure, muscle thickness, and patterns of fat distribution are inherited. The way your glands function was preset genetically when the Lord fashioned you in the womb. The kinds of food and exercise you need depend on your body structure.

Scientists have cataloged three general body types. *Endomorphs* are round and soft. They have small hands, wrists, and feet and carry most of their weight around the middle. They have poor muscle tone and tend to gain weight. Exercises like swimming, aerobic dancing, and calisthenics are best for endomorphs.

Ectomorphs are small-boned. They have lean, long necks, arms, and legs, and small chests and hips. They tend to slump, so many have poor posture. They thrive on fast-paced, endurance-type exercises, such as tennis, racquetball, cycling, and jogging.

Mesomorphs are muscular and big-boned. They have strong arms and legs and long necks. They have broad shoulders and large hips and chests. They're the "sporty" types who are good at and benefit from almost any kind of exercise, but they have to stick with it or pounds pile up.

YOU ARE WHAT YOU EAT

The kind of food you need—or shouldn't eat—also relates to your body type. Dr. Elliot D. Abravanel, author of *Body Type Diet and Lifetime Nutrition Plan,* classifies body types according to glandular function. He says pituitary types crave dairy products, which stimulate the pituitary gland but also put weight on. "In the thyroid type, cravings are for sweets and starches, which have long been known to stimulate the thyroid gland."[2] He states that the adrenal type craves animal products and salty foods; the gonadal type, spices and fats. He contends that eliminating or limiting what he calls "downfall foods" will cause weight loss.

"Foods that stimulate your dominant gland are the 'downfall foods' for your body type for they are the ones with the greatest power to undermine and sabotage your dieting efforts."[3] Knowing your body type can help you initiate and maintain an exercise and eating program.

GETTING THE INSIDE SCOOP

Examining your body's exterior or isolated symptoms will give you some knowledge of how your body works, but you also need a complete physical examination. Your personal physician is best qualified to tell you what's going on inside of your temple. Next time you go for your *annual* medical checkup, prepare a list of questions to ask. Find out exactly how high your blood pressure and cholesterol levels are and what you blood count is. (Do you know your blood type? That simple fact may save your life.) If your doctor prescribes any kind of medication, find out what it is for, what other drugs and foods it reacts to, and what side effects, if any, to expect. Ask for suggestions on how to improve your general health.

BEAUTIFYING THE TEMPLE

We're also responsible to maintain the exterior of the temple of the Holy Spirit, but Scripture warns that we shouldn't be preoccupied with it. Last year men and women in the United States spent over $21 billion on cosmetics and beauty aids. On the average, every adult in this country spends $6,123 a year on clothing and accessories. In 1983, more diet, exercise, and beauty books were published than any other nonfiction category. Many of us concentrate on pampering temporal externals rather than nurturing our souls. We neglect our "internal adornment" to which Peter referred as the hidden person of the heart (1 Peter 3:3–4).

Jesus taught that we should be more concerned for the welfare of our souls than our bodies. (See Matt. 10:28.) Actually, attending to the interior helps beautify the exterior. Proper sleep and rest, diet and exercise affect the condition of our skin, hair, and nails. At the same time, we want to look our best, we also want to make the gateway of our temple as appealing as possible. And we want to express our sexuality in God-honoring ways.

God gave each of us a temple, a human body that He fashioned with His hands. It's up to us to study it, understand it, and care for it. It's our responsibility to glorify God in our bodies and to make them appropriate dwelling places for the Holy Spirit.

WORKSHOP

I. Using a King James Version, look up the following Scriptures and write what the temple is called.
1. 2 Kings 11:10

2. Psalm 79:1

3. 1 Chronicles 29:2

4. 1 Chronicles 29:3

5. Isaiah 60:7

6. Isaiah 64:11

7. 2 Chronicles 20:8

8. John 2:16

Summarize what each of those titles infers about your body as a temple of the Holy Spirit.

II. Using a King James Version, look up the following passages and list the uses of the temple.

1. 1 Kings 8:10, 11, 13

2. 1 Kings 8:21

3. 2 Chronicles 2:4

4. 2 Kings 19:14–15

Summarize what these verses infer about the way you use and care for your body.

III. Answer the following questions to discover how well you know your body. If you don't know the answer, find it.
  1. Are you a night or morning person? How do you know? How can you use this to your advantage?

  2. How much sleep do you need to get rested and stay healthy? What happens to your body, mind, and emotions when you don't get enough sleep?

  3. Describe your basic metabolism.

4. What health problems might you have inherited? What are their basic symptoms? What can you do to minimize the chances of an occurrence?

5. If you're taking any kind of medication, describe exactly what it is supposed to do and its side effects.

6. What is your resting heart rate?

7. What is your blood pressure?

8. What is your blood type?

9. Do you suffer from any known allergies? If so, how do they affect you physically and emotionally?

10. What's your body type?

11. Outline an eating program that works for you. (Not just a diet to lose weight but a way of eating for health.)

12. Outline an exercise program that works for you.

IV. Name five things you can do to beautify the exterior of your temple.

Chapter Nine   A TIME FOR
                        EVERYTHING

"There is an appointed time for everything. And there is a time for every event under heaven" (Ecclesiastes 3:1).

Now let's talk about managing our time. When I was recently teaching a time-management seminar in the Midwest, a woman came up to me before I spoke and said, "For years I've been meaning to get my life organized but I've never been able to find the time. I hope this seminar helps." I assured her I hoped so, too.

After the first session ended, she hurried up to me and squealed, "It's helping! It's helping! This is the first time in my life I've actually thought about time and how I use it. Why didn't someone tell me this a long time ago?"

A great many of us are like that woman. We are so trapped by the tyranny of the immediate that we can't find time to put our lives in order. When we do think about time, it's generally because we're upset about how little of it we seem to have; however, if we consult a clock or a calendar, we find that each of us has the same number of hours in a day and days in the week. Dennis Hensley noted: "People relate to time in many different ways. Referees *call* time; prisoners *serve* time; musicians *mark* time; loafers *kill* time; statisticians *keep* time. But no matter how people relate to time, the fact remains that all of us are given the same amount of time. There are only 24 hours per day, 168 hours per week. Use them."[1]

A GIFT FROM GOD

Before we can properly manage time, we need to understand and appreciate it. We take time for granted because it's always there. We think of it as a nuisance. Oftentimes, it seems like clocks and schedules are our masters; other times, our enemies. Actually, time is a gift from God that gives balance, order, and meaning to life. Of all the gifts God has given us, we probably misuse and misunderstand time more than any other gift.

Have you ever thought what life would be like without time? Everything you do hinges on time. How did you know when to get up this morning, when to go to work, meet a friend for lunch, go to Bible study, fix dinner? Eliminating all of those o'clocks would be as chaotic as trying to play a game with no rules.

Time creates order in our lives. We don't have to guess when night will come or when the sun will rise. Scripture teaches "there is an appointed time for *everything*" (Eccl. 3:1). We make appointments, planning to be at specific places at specific times for definite reasons. Without the gift of time, we'd have to cancel all of life's appointments. There'd be no birthdays, no wedding anniversaries, no holidays. Time moves us in an orderly fashion from one event to the next.

We won't always be confined by time. There are no years, months, days, or hours in heaven. Time is a temporal gift; it is limited to this world. It is the opposite of eternal, which literally means to be set apart from time. God is eternal. He always has and always will exist in the present tense: His name is I AM, not I was or I will be. He is not controlled, limited, or affected by time because a thousand years are the same as a day to Him. So, there is no such thing as too fast or too slow for God. That's why we don't understand the Lord's timing and why it is difficult for us to think of time as a gift rather than a limitation.

A BIBLICAL PERSPECTIVE

The third chapter of Ecclesiastes contains some powerful observations about time. The entire passage is written in associated couplets—pairs of contrasting, complementary concepts—which gives it a sense of balance, order, and perspective. It offers insight into how we can accept and utilize the gift of time and how God operates within the sphere of time. In the loving hand of our sovereign Lord, there is a time for *every* event under heaven.

A TIME TO GIVE BIRTH—A TIME TO DIE

"There is a time to give birth, and a time to die" (Eccl. 3:2). We see God's scheduling in all of His creation. All living creatures have set gestation periods; we can't rush or change them. Unless there are complications, childbirth happens pretty much on schedule, and once those labor pains start, there's no way to reverse the process. Birth is inevitable.

So is death. An old adage says, when it's your time, you're going to go. In Psalm 139:16, David declared, "In Thy book they were all written, the days that were ordained *for me,* when as yet there was not one of them."

Our society shuns the idea of death. We don't even like to admit when someone dies. We avoid the word and say someone "passed away." Death is as much a part of life as birth, a part of God's perfect timing. As surely as we are born—and we had no say in when that would happen—we die. We cannot choose the time for that, either.

Remember the court battle and agonizing decision Karen Ann Quinlan's parents made several years ago? They chose to disconnect the life support systems that were sustaining their daughter. *They* pulled the plug, but the Lord had other plans. Karen Ann did not die until June, 1985.

Part of God's gift to us is the time He chooses for us to be born and to die. We are blessed by His perfect scheduling. Life is bracketed by fixed limits, birth and death, the duration is by His divine appointment.

A TIME TO PLANT—A TIME TO UPROOT

Next we read, there is "a time to plant, and a time to uproot what is planted" (Eccl. 3:2). This concept of sowing and reaping permeates all of God's creation. If you've ever planted a garden, you know that the package gives specific directions for planting the seeds. Some have to be sown after the last frost; some need to be in the ground all winter; and some must be planted in the spring; others in the fall. If the seeds are planted at the wrong time, they won't grow, and if they're uprooted or harvested too soon, they produce scrawny, immature, tasteless plants. For the peak in flavor and quality, planting and plucking must be done at the proper times.

This cycle can apply to plans. There is a time to perform and a time to abstain; a time to say yes and a time to say no. As Hugh Prather noted, "a time to *let* things happen and a time to *make* things happen."[2] In Hebrew, the word "plant" means to conceive, which implies there is a time for us to bear fruit, but there is also a time for us to be dormant. Judge Shirley M. Hufstedler observed, "The rhythm of life is intricate but orderly, tenacious but fragile. To keep that in mind is to hold the key to survival." Planting and uprooting are a lesson to us that we should fit into the flow and rhythm of life's normal, God-created time patterns.

A TIME TO KILL, HEAL, TEAR DOWN, BUILD UP

Some of the concepts in this particular passage of Scripture sound harsh, but they are realistic. Affirming that there is a time to kill sounds like a contradiction of the sixth commandment, "Thou shalt not kill" (Exod. 20:13). However, there are two Hebrew words used for the word "kill." The word used for kill in Exodus means premeditated murder, and the one in Ecclesiastes means to slay, cut down, or destroy. This can apply to various situations. In war, there is a time to kill the enemy. In government, there is a time to employ capital punishment. Sometimes, we destroy animals for food or to end their suffering.

Tearing down can apply to human relationships. In some instances, there is a time to sever a relationship. Some associations are so destructive or detrimental to one or both parties that it's best for everyone concerned if they terminate them, especially if it runs cross-grained with your Christianity. One of my daughter's friends, a recent Christian, just broke off a relationship with her boyfriend of five years because he's an unbeliever. This was a painful experience for them both, but it was something she was convinced she had to do. There *is* a time to tear down.

There is also a time to heal, which means to repair wounds. God uses us to bind up the broken-hearted and comfort and console those who are hurting. There's a time to dispense both tough and tender love. It's easier to repair wounds we haven't personally inflicted than to help heal hurt we've caused. Regardless of the source of the pains and problems in our ongoing relationships, there is a time to build up—to put aside anger and pride and bestow sympathy and mercy. We see this principle in action after a parent spanks a child and then offers hugs and kisses as an affirmation of love.

Tearing down and building up can also refer to our behavior patterns and habits. Paul said we are to "lay aside the old self" and "put on the new self" (Eph. 4:22, 24). There is a time to rid ourselves of the negatives in our lives. Conversely, there is a time for edification and for positive action.

A TIME TO WEEP, LAUGH, MOURN, DANCE

"There is a time to weep, and a time to laugh; a time to mourn, and a time to dance" (Eccl. 3:4). This verse makes three important statements about emotions. One, God expects us to have both positive and negative emotions: We will experience both joy and grief in life. Two, He expects us to express them: to laugh and dance when we are happy and cry and mourn when we are sad. The word "weep," as it is used in this verse, describes a deep, gutteral sobbing. "Mourn" means to make black, which is what grief does to our souls. The reactions portrayed in this verse are potent: soul-wrenching sobs, robust laughter, skipping around with glee. Third, sorrow is as legitimate as joy. God never promised or planned for us to be happy all of the time. There is a time to feel and express pain, as well as pleasure.

A TIME TO THROW AND GATHER STONES

Next, we learn there is "A time to throw stones, and a time to gather stones" (Eccl. 3:5). Throwing stones refers to a way of destroying land captured from an enemy in war, called the "scorched earth policy." 2 Kings 3:24–25 describes how this worked: "The Israelites arose and struck the Moabites, so that they fled before them; and they went forward into the land, slaughtering the Moabites. Thus they destroyed its cities; and each one threw a stone on every piece of good land and filled it. So they stopped all the springs of water and felled all the good trees."

After the earth was covered with stones, no one could build, plant, or live on it. Since it was uninhabitable, the people were forced to leave. The implication is that there is a time to bury the past and move on toward tomorrow. Yesterday is uninhabitable.

There is also a time to gather stones: to recoup our losses, make amends, and start over. Gathering stones is the opposite of giving up. There are times in life when we have to move on and begin again. Usually, such circumstances are forced on us by death, divorce, or financial reversals.

I will always remember the time I filled a position vacated by a widow who remarried. She hadn't the time to clean out her desk completely, so she asked me to put the rest of her belongings in a box she could pick up later. As I packed, I came across a slip of paper on which she'd neatly lettered: "You haven't lived until you've had to start over!" She'd written it shortly after the death of her first husband. She definitely had a sense of God's timing.

A TIME TO EMBRACE AND SHUN EMBRACING

Next, the Preacher tell us, there is "a time to embrace, and a time to shun embracing" (Eccl. 3:5). Embrace means to grasp closely. There is a time to cling to what we're doing and a time to turn loose. Knowing when to persist or when to quit takes wisdom. In our society, we frown on quitting and consider it a form of failure; in God's economy, there *is* a time to give up. Many times, refusing to give up is a tremendous waste of time. We refer to it as "spinning our wheels" or "pounding our heads against a brick wall." Some things get us nowhere and should be abandoned as futile and fruitless.

Luke recounts the time when Jesus and the disciples were on their way to Jerusalem. It was late in the afternoon. Everyone was hot and tired. The Lord sent some of the men ahead to a Samaritan village to find a place for the group to stay, but no one would offer them lodging because they were Jews. James and John were incensed when the villagers denied their request. They weren't about to let the matter drop. They said, "Lord, do You want us to command fire to come down from heaven and consume them?" (Luke 9:54).

In that moment, Jesus shunned embracing. He knew it was time to quit. The Word states simply, "He turned and rebuked them . . . and they went on to another village" (Luke 9:55–56).

We see two principles about timing in these verses. One is that nothing goes on forever: Life is always fluctuating, never static. The one thing we can be certain of in life is change. The other principle is that neither throwing or gathering stones, nor embracing or shunning embracing are absolutes. They operate interchangeably. In the course of our lives, we will be clinging to certain things as we are releasing others.

A TIME TO SEARCH AND GIVE UP AS LOST

The next observation about time, there is "a time to search, and a time to give up as lost" (Eccl. 3:6), applies to *actions*. Most things don't come easily, so most people have to seek after happiness, pursue goals, and work hard to achieve success. The great achievements in life usually are the result of hard work and perseverance. Ralph Waldo Emerson noted, "Shallow men believe in luck, believe in circumstances. Strong men believe in cause and effect." Searching is the cause that brings the effect of positive results.

Sometimes, no matter how hard we try or how industriously and zealously we pursue a goal, things don't work out. We reach a point where giving up as lost is the only sensible and realistic course of action. Then, we throw our hands up in the air and say, "That's it! I'm through!" Quitting is wrong only if we don't move on to something else, if we don't start a new search.

Note that giving up is always preceded by searching. There's a difference between quitting and being a quitter. Quitters don't try. They give up for the wrong reasons or before they've exercised all logical options. People who know when to quit are realists, who recognize that there is a time to give up as lost.

A TIME TO KEEP AND A TIME TO THROW AWAY

The next admonition, there is "a time to keep and a time to throw away," refers to *ideas* (Eccl. 3:6). None of us is right all of the time. We all harbor some misconceptions while our other ideas and opinions are right on target. We like to cling to pet theories, even erroneous ones.

I compare this keeping and discarding of ideas to cleaning out a closet. Every fall and spring, I sort through my wardrobe. I throw away clothes that are worn out or no longer in fashion. Then, I store the rest to use again next season. There's a time to do that with our beliefs and opinions.

Robert Munger in a sermon "My Heart Christ's Home," explains how Christ can help us decide which thoughts to save and which ones to throw out: "In my home [the study of my mind] is a very small room with very thick walls. But it is an important room. In a sense, it is the control room of the house. He entered with me. . . . There was a lot of trash and literature on the table that a Christian had no business reading and as for the pictures on the wall—the imaginations and thoughts of my mind—these were shameful.

"I turned to Him and said, 'Master, I know this room needs a radical alteration. Will you help me make it what it ought to be—to bring every thought into captivity to you?'

'Surely!' He said. 'Gladly I will help you.'"

Surely our Lord knows which thoughts we should keep and which we should throw away.

A TIME TO TEAR APART AND SEW— TO BE SILENT AND TO SPEAK

At first glance, the next couplets, there is "a time to tear apart, and sew together; a time to be silent, and a time to speak" (Eccl. 3:7), appear to be unassociated. What does sewing have to do with talking? Actually, this verse is a description of how God expects us to cope with the death of loved ones and an affirmation of how time heals. Tearing apart refers to the ancient custom of ripping garments when devastating events or death occurred. It is part of the mourning process spoken of in verse four. It's an intense, immediate, though brief, response to grief.

Ultimately, this initial, overt reaction makes sense. When tragedy strikes, most people feel like kicking, screaming, and hitting to tear at the grief that overwhelms them. The idea of tearing apart is contrary to the give-them-a-tranquilizer-to-dull-reality approach that many people use today. There is a time to express sorrow overtly. Doing so doesn't show a lack of faith nor does it mean a person is hysterical. It is natural and normal to weep and lose control, then lapse into shocked silence.

Tragedy and adversity cause us to withdraw, to turn our thoughts inward and meditate. There is a time to be silent, to sort through quiet remembrances, to think about the person who is gone, to think about the ramifications of a situation, and to digest the immensity of what has happened and the effect it will have on our lives. These two reactions, tearing apart and being silent, help us work through pain and face reality. They are part of God's formula for healing.

After a while, it's time to move beyond the initial grief. There comes a time to sew together and speak. As we do, recovery begins. Eventually, we emerge from the intensity and silence of sorrow and pull together the broken fragments to start reweaving the fabric of life.

A TIME TO LOVE AND A TIME TO HATE

The phrase "a time to love and a time to hate" relates to interpersonal relationships. This is another of those seemingly contradictory verses. Scripture clearly teaches that hatred is a sin. Jesus said, "You have heard that it was said,

'You shall love your neighbor, and hate your enemy. But I say to you, love your enemies" (Matt. 5:43). Obviously, acknowledging that there is a time to hate doesn't mean that we are supposed to, but that we will. There are times when this kind of deep-seated animosity will exist. When it does, we have to admit what we are feeling, then obey the law of Christ and subdue it with love. Love should be an ever-present, active element in our lives; hatred should be passive. Just because it is present doesn't mean we have to respond to it.

This couplet can also refer to loving righteousness and hating sin. Paul said we should "abhor what is evil; cling to what is good" (Rom. 12:9). Regardless of whether a time to hate is a reference to a negative emotion or a positive reaction to sin, there always comes a time to love, which erases the eroding effects of hatred.

A TIME FOR WAR AND A TIME FOR PEACE

The final couplet, "a time for war, and a time for peace" (Eccl. 3:8), is an observation about world affairs. As abhorrent as the prospect is, there *is* a time for war. Throughout the Old Testament, God's people fought against evil and the Lord's enemies. In World War II, freedom-loving nations fought the insidious evils perpetrated by Hitler and his allies. But eventually, there comes a time for peace. Peace, not war, is God's ideal. Scripture encourages us to pursue peace. Christ called Christians peacemakers. The fact that there is a time for war does not justify viewing it as a solution that is superior to peace.

The message in Ecclesiastes is clear. Time is a divinely ordained gift from God; it is the framework that provides limits and boundaries for our lives. "Time is a versatile performer. It flies, marches on, heals all wounds, runs out and will tell."[3] Appreciating and understanding the value of every moment God allots us is the first step toward successful time management.

WORKSHOP

I. The concept of appointed time is beautifully illustrated in the creation story. Read the verses listed below and list what was created.

   1. Genesis 1:3–4

   2. Genesis 1:6–7

   3. Genesis 1:9–10

   4. Genesis 1:11

   5. Genesis 1:14

   6. Genesis 1:20

   7. Genesis 1:24

   8. Genesis 1:27

II. Based on the verses you have just read, answer the following questions.

   1. Why did the Lord create day, night, the atmosphere and dry land and water before He created plants and seasons?

   2. What do sea animals and birds eat? How does this relate to their order in creation?

   3. What do creeping things and larger animals and beasts eat? How does this relate to their order in creation?

4. Why do you suppose God created man and woman last?

III. Write your definition of time.

IV. List three of your most difficult "time" problems.

Chapter Ten

NUMBERING YOUR DAYS

"Teach us to number our days and recognize how few they are; help us to spend them as we should" (Psalm 90:12 LB).

If you're like most people, you don't think much about numbers, yet all of us use them constantly: Every time we address a letter, dial the telephone, shop, figure the balance in our checkbook, plan a dinner party, write a charge account number on our check when we pay a bill, or when we consult a calendar, we use numbers. Numbers are a necessity of life and in multitudes of ways, contribute order and meaning to everything we do. They delineate quantity, for example, we know we'll get twelve eggs when we buy a dozen or how many tickets to sell to fill the seats in a concert hall. They help us measure and manage time: We know there are twenty-four hours in a day, seven days in each week, fifty-two weeks in every year.

David understood how numbers help us structure and use time. Thousands of years ago, he prayed, "Teach us to number our days and recognize how few they are; help us to spend them as we should" (Ps. 90:12 LB). Numbering our days involves setting up an orderly, enjoyable, workable daily routine that brings us personal satisfaction, propels us toward our goals, and helps us accomplish all we want and need to accomplish. In modern terminology, numbering our days means establishing priorities for how we will use time. That kind of structuring is an absolute necessity for successful time management.

Unfortunately, many of us spend the better part of each

day involved in a morass of meaningless, unnecessary activity. There are several reasons why we have difficulty pinpointing and establishing priorities. One is that we unthinkingly become involved in so many things that we immobilize ourselves. Most of us tend to take on more than we can handle. We find ourselves feverishly active, accomplishing very little. We're faced with so many "have tos" that we don't have time for the "want tos" or "fun tos," we reach a point where there isn't room to cram one more thing into our overcrowded schedules. Being overly involved restricts our freedom of choice and saddles us with an interminable number of unnecessary duties.

THE RUT OF ROUTINE

Another reason we have difficulty establishing priorities is because we get locked into routines, which soon become habits, which soon become a way of life. We don't evaluate how we do things or if there's a more efficient, time-effective way to do them. People who are stuck in the rut of routine live and die by the slogan, "But I've always done it this way."

For years, I did my grocery shopping on Friday morning after I went to the bank. And for years, I complained when I had to go to the market again on Monday because we'd always run out of something over the weekend. When I thought about it, I decided that shopping on Friday wasn't a good idea, so I started doing my weekly marketing on Monday. Changing the way I'd always done it saved me time and money, not to mention aggravation. It freed Fridays for me to work, and I'm buying groceries once a week, instead of twice.

Routines should serve a purpose. Prioritizing helps us evaluate and restructure our routines.

FAULTY FOCUSING

The main reason we have difficulty discerning and setting up priorities is because we focus our attention on things that aren't God's will for us. Many times we operate somewhere to the left of the center of God's perfect will simply because we didn't consult the Lord about how to spend and invest our time. The problem of faulty focusing isn't unique to our culture; it's ageless. A woman who was a close friend of Christ's had this problem, and the Lord used a personal encounter with her to teach an important lesson about priorities.

Jesus and His disciples had been traveling around the countryside, teaching and ministering. They were, no doubt, exhausted when they arrived at the village of Bethany and looked forward to a home-cooked meal and a good night's sleep. Jesus frequently secluded Himself there at the home of His friends, Mary, Martha, and Lazarus. Luke 10:38 tells us that when He arrived, "Martha welcomed Him into her home."

Martha was hospitable. I'm sure she felt privileged that the Lord would choose her home as a place to recuperate and refresh Himself. Making her guests comfortable was a priority for her. Being a good hostess would require a great deal of behind-the-scenes preparation, especially if the guests were unexpected, as they may have been in this instance. The fact that Jesus chose to stay at her place says a lot about the kind of home it was. He obviously enjoyed both the atmosphere and the company.

Obviously, Martha had a lot to do. While she was hustling about, getting the house ready and fixing dinner, her sister Mary "was listening to the Lord's word, seated at His feet" (Luke 10:39).

MARY'S PRIORITY

Mary's priority was listening to Jesus. They weren't merely carrying on polite conversation; He was teaching her. We take this privilege for granted, but Mary wasn't. In her culture, women were considered intellectually inferior, incapable of in-depth learning. She wasn't about to pass up an opportunity to receive firsthand instruction from the Lord. I doubt that she was even aware of what was going on around her.

MARTHA'S PRIORITY

The opposite was true with Martha. She was so involved that she was distracted with all of her preparations. She was so concerned for the comfort of her guests, she became so wrapped up in what she was doing that her activity distracted her from the Lord. Her focus was faulty; her priorities were out of order.

Sound like anyone you know? Which of us hasn't let the everyday hustle and bustle of life distract us from the Lord? All of us, at one time or another, have become so involved in *what* we're doing that we forget *who* we're doing it for.

I can understand how Martha felt. Most women have been in her place sometime in their lives. They're stuck in the kitchen doing all of the work while everyone else socializes in the living room. I can imagine what Martha was saying to herself, *This isn't fair . . . Mary doesn't care . . . she's taking advantage of me. I'm always the one who does most of the work.* The more Martha thought about it, the angrier she got. Finally, she was so disgruntled by Mary's seeming lack of concern, she couldn't keep silent any longer. She had to say something.

MARTHA'S ACCUSATION

I can visualize Martha sashaying out of the kitchen, planting herself firmly in front of the Lord, and placing her hands on her hips (probably because that's what I'd have done). I think she ignored Mary and spoke directly to the Lord because she knew her sister was listening to Jesus and would do anything He asked. She assumed if He told Mary to help in the kitchen, she would.

Martha certainly wasn't polite or gracious at that moment. She accused Jesus of being uncaring and of not appreciating her efforts. Then before He had a chance to answer, she told Him what to do. She said, "Lord, do you not care that my sister has left me to do all the serving alone? Then tell her to help me" (Luke 10:40).

Obviously, Martha had decided that she knew better than the Lord or Mary what her sister's priority should be. Martha thought Mary should be helping her serve rather than sitting at the Lord's feet.

We're a lot like Martha, too. We take it upon ourselves to tell God what to do. We judge how others, especially the people closest to us, should use their time. We expect their priorities to match ours. When they don't, we get angry and feel used and unappreciated. We criticize what they do when actually our own priorities are the ones out of focus. When that happens, God's will for our lives becomes fuzzy, like a photograph taken with an improperly focused camera. We lose sight of what's important; we get sidetracked by things that don't matter.

MARTHA'S BASIC PROBLEM

I think Jesus chuckled slightly when He answered Martha's complaint. "Martha, Martha," He began. When the Lord repeats a name in Scripture, He does it to emphasize a point, to get a person's attention, and to show affection and concern. Although Jesus rebuked Martha, He did it gently with a touch of humor.

Never one to mince words, He immediately pointed out Martha's basic problem. He said, "You are worried and bothered about so many things" (Luke 10:41). In that respect we're all a bit like Martha, aren't we? We all waste time, energy, and emotions fussing, fuming, and fretting. Yet, as Jesus reasoned, "Who of you by worrying can add a single hour to his life?" (Matt. 6:27 NIV). Worry is unworthwhile. It can make havoc of priorities because we try to alleviate the anxiety it causes rather than to seek God's will. That's what happened to Martha. She wasn't thinking about what God wanted her to do, or what would be best for her, but what Jesus and Mary should be doing to relieve her stress.

GODLY ADVICE ABOUT PRIORITIES

After the Lord pointed out Martha's basic problem, He gave her some advice about establishing priorities. He said, "only a few things are necessary" (Luke 10:42). What a relief to know that from God's perspective, only a few things in life are necessary or deserve intense attention and concern. Jesus' counsel to Martha makes as much sense for us as it did for her. Most of us have so many priorities that we're weighted down by the sheer bulk of them. John W. Alexander expressed a sentiment many of us experience: "One of the most frustrating feelings in life is to awaken to a new day and face so many tasks that we are overwhelmed by their magnitude."[1]

Jesus cautioned against overloading our minds and schedules with an excess of unnecessary things. Most of the things we get worked up over aren't that important in the overall scheme of our lives. Many of the things we worry about never happen, or if they do, they don't have the kind of catastrophic results we'd imagined. Most of you can't reflect back a week and remember what anxieties swallowed your time, sapped your mental energy, distorted your emotions, or infringed on your happiness and peace of mind. Could you name the specific things that worried and bothered you six weeks ago today? Chances are you couldn't.

Remember, only a few things are necessary. This can help us pinpoint priorities. As we prioritize, we must ask ourselves, *Is this necessary? Is this worth being concerned about? Is this worth being incorporated into our lives?*

ONE NECESSARY THING!

After the Lord told Martha only a few things were necessary, He qualified His statement even further. He said, "Really *only* one, for Mary has chosen the good part which shall not be taken away from her" (Luke 10:42). Christ's counsel to Martha included an important time-management principle: *There is only one thing God wants us doing at any given moment.* His will for us as individuals should always be our priority. We discover what that is when we follow Mary's example and spend time with the Lord, instead of running ourselves ragged trying to get everything done. God wants to direct every aspect of our lives, including the way we use our time. We have to "foot-sit" before we can discern His will.

The Lord has plans for each of us, things He has preordained for us to do that will bring blessing and fulfillment. " 'I know the plans I have for you,' declares the Lord, 'plans for welfare and not calamity to give you a future and a hope'" (Jer. 29:11). He knows what is best for us and what our priorities should be because He knows the future. When we place ourselves at His feet and relinquish our time to Him, He shows us what is necessary and what isn't and what our personal priorities should be.

THE IMPORTANCE OF FOOT-SITTING

Too often, we *find* time to spend with the Lord rather than *make* time for Him; we treat Him as an afterthought rather than as our first priority; and we turn to Him only when we have problems or need His help. Jesus said, "Seek *first* [God's] kingdom and His righteousness and all these things shall be added to you" (Matt. 6:33). God deserves better than to be sandwiched in between church meetings, television programs, and dirty dishes.

Foot-sitting is more than praying and reading the Bible for fifteen minutes every morning. It is maintaining constant communication with Christ: perpetually spreading our daily schedules and activities before Him and consulting Him before we do anything. When we plant ourselves firmly at His feet and listen to Him, we're able to discern His will, pinpoint personal priorities, and properly number our days.

DISCERNING GOD'S WILL

Some Christians try all kinds of shortcuts to discover God's will for how they should use their time. One shortcut frequently used I call the "Open-door Theory." This erroneous bit of theology is one of my pet peeves because it severely interferes with the way people manage their time and keeps them from actively numbering their days. It goes something like this: When God wants me to do something, He simply makes His will known through the opportunities that come my way.

Just last week, a young man told me he had taken a new job assignment "because the Lord opened the door, so I knew it was His will." I asked him why he was so certain the Lord had opened that particular door. He admitted to me that he hadn't done any foot-sitting nor had he prayed or logically thought through the move. He had assumed because the promotion had come along, God wanted him to take it.

There are several problems with the Open-door Theory. One is that it keeps us from working through alternatives with the Lord. Another is that it presumes that doing God's will will be easy, that is, there won't be any obstacles in our paths if we're in tune with God's desires for our lives. I'm certain Paul would disagree with that simplistic approach. Several of his open doors led to prison cells.

The Open-door Theory is also grounded in the false belief that God directs us primarily through external circumstances rather than through the desires He implants in our hearts. This is the direction of the indwelling Holy Spirit and the guidance we glean when we foot-sit. Scripture warns us to "examine everything carefully" (1 Thess. 5:21). That includes open doors.

Another fallacy embodied in the Open-door Theory is the assumption that every opportunity that crosses our paths was sent by the Lord. It presumes that if a door is open, we're automatically obligated to walk through it. That isn't so. It may be God's will that we stay outside. In Acts 16, Luke tells how the Holy Spirit forbade Paul "to speak the word in Asia" at that specific time. The Lord sometimes leads us *not* to do things. Adhering to this fallacy means we are walking by fact, not by faith.

Another fault with the Open-door Theory is that it presumes we will never be presented with more than one opportunity at a time. Many times in my life I've been faced with several open doors simultaneously. Each sheltered a good thing that could have been God's will for me; each presented an opportunity for me to work, serve, minister, and use and develop my talents. The Open-door Theory is useless under such circumstances.

Also, this theory makes God totally responsible for revealing His will to us, instead of making us responsible to discern it. It keeps us from thinking and praying about what the Lord wants and what would be best for us.

GROUND RULES FOR NUMBERING
OUR DAYS

Revealing His will to us is God's responsibility; seeking it is ours. But knowing His will isn't enough. Once we discern it, we have to do it. Let's look at six ground rules that can help us number our days.

The first is to *decide which of your priorities are out of focus.* It's easy to get sidetracked from God's perfect will by doing good things. Martha was hospitable: She wanted to make her guests comfortable and serve a good meal. Those are good things but they distorted Martha's priorities.

If I accept a speaking engagement to teach a seminar in Florida and God wants me in Granada Hills with my family at that time, I would not be doing His perfect will if I go. I would be doing a good thing—something that could help the people who attend the seminar, something that is part of the career the Lord has given me—but not the *one* thing He wants me doing at that particular time. My priorities would be out of focus.

William E. Gladstone noted, "There is a limit to the work that can be got out of human body or a human brain, and he is wise who wastes no energy on pursuits for which he is not fitted; and he is still wiser who, from among the things that he can do well, chooses and resolutely follows the best." We must continuously foot-sit to discern what to pursue resolutely, as well as what noble deeds will sidetrack us from God's perfect will. Sometimes, I think we're more easily led astray by honorable, though misdirected, intentions than we are by overt sin. The *good* things are the most difficult to spot because they *are* good.

Announce Your Intentions

Ground rule two for numbering your days is to *announce your intention to establish priorities.* Tell your friends and family, and possibly your employer, what you're doing and why. Ask for their help, patience, and prayers. You'll be making changes in your life that will affect them, too, so they need to know what's happening.

When I decided to free-lance out of my home, I told my friends that I'd be keeping office hours, the same as if I went out to work every day. I asked them to make social phone calls to me before 8 A.M. or after 4 P.M. My friends actually became a support group that helped me stick to my new time priorities.

Decide What You Want To Do

The third ground rule for numbering your days is to *decide what you want to accomplish*. Set goals: Determine what you want to achieve today, this week, this month, this season, this year, five years from now, during your lifetime. Edwin Bliss says, "Goals should be attainable and authentic . . . things you really want and are willing to work for."[2]

Having definite goals helps to pinpoint priorities. For example, although I wasn't always consciously aware of it, writing a novel is one of my lifetime goals. That eventually motivated me to establish certain priorities: to have a completed manuscript ready to present to a publisher by a certain year, to hire a literary agent to market it when it's finished, to do the final draft and research for the novel by next fall, to edit a chapter a week, and to spend at least one hour every day working on the book.

I needed to set a goal—to write a novel—before I could prioritize the activities that would help me accomplish it. That's true with anything we do.

What's Important

Ground rule four for numbering your days is to *decide what's important to you*. Don't devote yourself exclusively to the "have tos" or "should tos." Don't let other people establish your priorities for you.

Being home with my children always has been an

important priority to me, so I have structured my career accordingly. It wasn't a matter of right or wrong but a personal desire to be with my children. I established that priority for my own peace of mind because being with them during their formative years was so important to me.

Prioritize Time Demands

The fifth ground rule is to *weigh the priority of every time demand* that crosses your path. Dru Scott, Ph.D., noted: "Time demands don't march into your life in orderly ranks, waving banners with preassigned priorities. Most often they resemble an unruly mob, crowding in at once and competing for your time and attention. Even though you know it isn't possible, they may all seem to be waving banners that say, 'I'm the most important.' Every time a demand in that unruly mob calls for your attention, consider what priority it really should have *right now.*"[3]

When that "unruly mob" attacks, you don't have to surrender. Don't cave in under the coercion of the immediate. Instead, ask yourself: Is this necessary? Is it something that has to be done now? At all? By me? Is it truly an emergency? Judge Shirley M. Hufstedler observed, "There is much in life that doesn't have to be done instantly. There are phone calls that don't have to be returned immediately. There are many difficult problems and decisions that actually improve when they are left to simmer a little while."

We'd all do well to heed the advice Lord Chesterfield gave his son: "I recommend you take care of the minutes, for the hours will take care of themselves."[4] Minor time demands won't snowball into big ones if we weigh them carefully and thoughtfully and keep them in their proper perspective.

Plan Each Day

The sixth and final ground rule for establishing priorities is to *plan each day*. In his book *Managing Our Work,* John W. Alexander defines planning as "deciding in advance what should be done, *why* it should be done, *where* it should be done, *when* it should be done and *how* it should be done."[5] I'd add two more aspects: *if* it should be done and *who* should do it.

We can't settle for establishing priorities once a year, once a month, once a week, or even once a day; they must be thought through several times throughout the day. We need to plan each day and prioritize within it because every day is different. Each brings its own set of time demands, challenges, and changes. In their book *Catch a Red Leaf*, Gladis and Gordon DePree noted: "We would not think of wearing the same clothing every day, or eating the same food every day, or even repeating the same words every day to the people we meet. Every day is different, and some days we dress up or dress down, we eat more or less, we exchange appropriate words. To do exactly what we did yesterday might be terribly inappropriate."[6]

THE TRAUMA OF TRIVIA

Numbering our days means constantly sifting through the events in our lives to make us more aware of what's happening. We live such active, demanding lives that it's easy to lose sight of the total picture and let irrelevant, unimportant activities consume great chunks of our time. Dr. Dru Scott notes that, "many people feel that effective time management begins with the trivial concerns . . . Not so . . . [they] have the least value in terms of contributing to what you want most. That's why those jobs deserve the lowest priority."[7]

Our neighbor sweeps the gutter around her house every morning. (No, I am not joking!) The wife of a man George works with literally manicures her front lawn: Every week she washes the leaves of certain plants with a cloth and trims her prize flowers with scissors. Carol irons her sheets. Diane vacuums her entire five-bedroom house every day because she read somewhere that dirt will make the carpet wear out faster. Kathy won't let her husband and children do dishes because they don't load the dishwasher properly and they splash water on the floor. What these people do is their business, but all but one of them has complained to me about how busy she is. Each is a master at "trivial pursuit." Yet, not one of those things I mentioned contributes to the overall quality of their lives.

William E. Gladstone said, "To comprehend a man's life, it is necessary to know not merely what he does but also what he purposely leaves undone." Prioritizing helps us determine what to do, as well as what *not* to do. Numbering our days protects us from the trauma of trivia.

Suggestions for Prioritizing

If you're like me, you need a definite plan of action to help you prioritize. Here are some suggestions that have proven helpful to me.

1. Every day, spend fifteen minutes conversing with the Lord on a personal level: Foot-sit. This is in addition to your regular praying or Bible reading and study; it is a time when you sit and talk with Him like you do with your husband or your best friend.

2. Every day, do one thing to help you reach a goal. It needn't be a major undertaking, just something that moves you toward the fulfillment of a future dream.

3. Every day, do one unexpected, unrequired thing for someone you love, an above-and-beyond something that will bless them and show you care in a special, intimate way.

4. Every day, do yourself a favor; pamper yourself in some way. The philosopher Goethe recommended, "One ought everyday at least, to hear a little song, read a good poem, see a fine picture and, if possible, speak a few reasonable words." Take a walk. Make a long-distance phone call to a friend who lives out of state. Give yourself a pedicure. Start reading that book that's been sitting on the shelf for six months.

5. Every day, do one thing you've been putting off. You may not complete a project, but at least you'll get started and can finish a portion of the whole. Work at it, a little at a time, until it's done.

A line from "Look to This Day" in the *Sanskrit* notes, "Today well lived makes every yesterday a dream of happiness and every tomorrow a vision of hope. Look well, therefore, to this day." Numbering our days—pinpointing and establishing priorities and working toward goals—helps us look well to each day and do that one thing at every given moment that is God's perfect will.

WORKSHOP

1. Write your definition of priorities.

2. Ask three other people their definition of priorities and write their answers.

    a.

    b.

    c.

3. Are you immobilized by involvement or traumatized by trivia? On a separate sheet of paper, make a list of all of your time commitments, including those to your family. Put a " **+** " by the ones you have to do. (This means there is no way you cannot do them and that no one else could do them.) Put a "*" by the ones you do because you want to. Put an "X" by the things you dislike doing, but feel forced to do. Put a "T" by trivia that is a waste of time. Draw a line through the things you could or should drop—areas where you are involved and don't need to be or shouldn't be. What does your list tell you about your priorities? What can you do to free yourself from certain involvements?

4. Are you stuck in the rut of routine? In the space below, list five major jobs you do as part of your daily or weekly routine. Think about how you do them and write one way you could do each more efficiently.

    a.

b.

c.

d.

e.

5. Are your priorities out of focus? In column A, make a list of your priorities. Present them to the Lord. Spend several days talking with Him about them. Ask Him to show you His perfect will concerning each priority. After you foot-sit, revise your priority list from column A into an new list in column B.

Column A	Column B

6. What are your goals? Fill in the spaces.

a. List three lifetime goals, things you want to accomplish in your lifetime.

b. List three long-range goals for each lifetime goal, things you should plan to do in the next two to three years that will help you reach your lifetime goals.

c. List three intermediate goals for each long-range goal, things you need to do in the next three to six months to work toward your long-range goals.

d. Now list immediate goals, things you must do today, tomorrow, and next week to fulfill your intermediate goals. (*Hint:* Your immediate goals should help you reach your intermediate ones, which should help you reach long-range ones, which should move you toward lifetime goals.) These immediate goals are more detailed than any others and need to be prioritized as activities into your daily schedule.

Chapter Eleven

THE ECOLOGY
OF TIME

"See then that ye walk circumspectly, not as fools, but as wise, redeeming the time, because the days are evil" (Ephesians 5:15–16 KJV).

The letter began, "Dear Mrs. Berry, Several months ago I bought your tapes on time management, but I have a real problem. I cannot find time to listen to them. Can you suggest something I can do to carve out three extra hours? Right now I don't have three extra minutes. I am desperate and would appreciate an *immediate* reply!"

The woman who wrote that letter is an example of what can happen if we do not learn to ecologize our time. Ecology is the science that deals with the relationships between organisms and their environment. Time management is the "science" that deals with the relationship between people and time. Ecology-conscious people are concerned with preserving and conserving our natural resources. Ecological researchers are always trying to find new and better ways to conserve and distribute natural resources. Similarly, I like to think of time management as the field of knowledge that involves finding new and better ways to conserve, safeguard, and distribute that precious commodity—time.

Of all the natural resources God has given us, we probably misuse time more than any other. And like other resources, when we thoughtlessly consume it, we create a shortage. Time-management expert Peter Drucker has said, "Time is a unique resource. No matter how high the demand, the supply will not go up. It is totally perishable and cannot be stored. Nothing can substitute for it."

Time is invaluable, but we carelessly waste it. We don't leave faucets running when we finish showering or use lights when the sun brightly illumines a room. We don't leave the motor idling when the car is in the garage for the night. Yet, we let minutes slip by without taking notice of where they have gone or how we have used them.

GOD'S FORMULA FOR REDEEMING TIME

Genesis 1:14 states that God created time—day, night, the seasons, the years. In Ephesians 5:15–16, Paul gave us a formula for how to be ecologically sound in the way we use our time. "See then that ye walk circumspectly, not as fools but as wise, redeeming the time, because the days are evil" (KJV).

God's formula for time management contains three specific principles: walk circumspectly, be wise, and redeem the time. The admonition to walk circumspectly is a warning that literally means *be careful how you live!* We must thoughtfully and carefully invest our time, so we'll receive the greatest return on the minutes and hours God has granted each of us.

Walk Wisely

The second principle in God's formula for redeeming time is to *walk wisely*. In the biblical sense, wisdom is insight, an ability to discern how to use knowledge coupled with an understanding of the consequences of actions. God expects us to be smart about the way we use our time. We must view our lives globally, deciding how to conserve and distribute every minute He allots us, so we redeem, rather than waste or misuse, our time.

Redeem the Time

The basic, underlying principle in the formula is to *redeem the time*. Redeeming time means "making the most of every opportunity and turning each [moment] to the best advantage."[1] If you're like me, you're always looking for bargains.

One of the ways I save money on my weekly grocery bill is by redeeming coupons. Every Thursday, I go through all of the mail flyers and the food section of the *Los Angeles Times*. I clip out manufacturers' cents-off coupons and file them in a recipe box that I carry to the store with me. Most of the local supermarkets offer two or three double coupons every week, as well as cents-off coupons of their own. Last week, I had a coupon for fifty cents off my family's favorite brand of catsup. It was also on special at my market. Using a double coupon with a manufacturer's coupon, I got a thirty-two ounce bottle of catsup for fourteen cents.

Redeeming coupons is a great way to conserve and reclaim cash. It's making the most of every cent spent on food. Redeeming the time is making the most of every moment we spend. We conserve, plan, and carefully watch how we use our time.

God's formula for redeeming time ends with a warning: "because the days are evil" (Eph. 5:16). It's as if the Lord is telling us that redeeming the time will take effort; it won't be easy, and we'll have to work at it well. There are so many forces making demands on our time. Satan, appearing as an angel of light, tempts us to do good things that aren't God's will for our lives. People we love demand and need our attention. There are always more jobs to be done than we can do. It's easy to get sidetracked or to forget to foot-sit or to let habit take over, instead of expending the extra effort that proper time management requires.

HOW DO YOU USE YOUR TIME?

Understanding how we use our time can help us learn how to redeem it. All time-management experts agree that we must have some system of categorizing the way we use time. You can devise your own classifications or use the ones I suggest. I divide time consumption into seven categories: *vital, immediate, emergencies, good-and-necessary, good-but-unnecessary, busy work,* and *wasted time.* The *vital* category is the most important. It involves things that are conducive to personal growth, that build self-esteem, that generate well-being, and that help us reach lifelong goals. This category includes activities that alter and improve the course and overall quality of our lives. Many things that are extremely important are not urgent, so we neglect them, such as taking the class that will guarantee a promotion, having an annual physical or dental checkup, studying the Bible daily, losing fifteen pounds, updating our house insurance policy or our legal will. The *vital* category deserves the most attention but usually gets the least.

Many people confuse urgency and importance. Michael LeBoeuf, author of *Working Smart,* cautions that we must learn to distinguish between the two. He says, "When you are faced with a number of problems, ask yourself which ones are the truly important ones, and make them your first priority. If you allow yourself to be governed by what's urgent, your life will be one crisis after another."[2] You'll be controlled by circumstances, whereas concentrating on what's vital will help you use your time both wisely and well.

Immediate Activities and Emergencies

The *immediate* category includes those ever-present, life-sustaining maintenance activities that have to be done in the everyday course of life: brushing teeth, filling the car with gas, filing income tax, shopping for clothes and food, eating. Immediate activities seldom cause time-management problems because they're part of our daily routine and *have* to be done. Usually, they have deadlines. You brush teeth when you get up in the morning and before you go to bed. You get gas when the gauge edges toward empty. You file tax returns by April 15. You buy clothes when you need them and eat when you are hungry.

Emergencies, the third category of time usage, don't cause many time-management problems either. They don't happen very often, and when they do, they have to be handled as soon as they occur. Emergencies don't need to be managed; they demand to be done. They scramble our schedules but don't interfere with priorities because, by nature, an emergency *is* a number-one priority.

The basic difference between immediate activities and emergencies is that you can procrastinate, to a certain extent, on the former but not the latter. If your car gets a flat tire, you don't debate whether or not to wait until a week from Tuesday to get it fixed. If you chip a tooth, you don't wait until your next checkup to go to the dentist. If the sink springs a leak, you don't schedule an appointment with the plumber the following week. Generally, emergencies cause an abundance of inconvenience but few time-management problems.

Those Good-and-Necessary Items

The fourth time-usage category is *good-and-necessary.* These are things we enjoy and want to do. They contribute to our pleasure and personal gratification, as well as the welfare of others. Good and necessary activities aren't mandatory, but they enrich our lives. Leisure and recreational activities, hobbies, and vacations fall into this category. Our family didn't have to go to Wyoming last summer, but our trip was good and necessary. We enjoyed the awesome beauty of God's creation in Yellowstone National Park and the Grand Teton Mountains. We had an absolute ball together on a whitewater-rapids trip. We experienced rich Christian fellowship with each other and my niece and her family. And we came home rested and refreshed.

Sometimes, people confuse leisure time with wasting time, but they aren't the same. Leisure means taking time for rest, recuperation, recreation, and for replenishing our bodies, minds, and spirits. It is the time we invest in pleasures that restore the soul, whether reading a book, listening to music, visiting with a friend, exercising, climbing a mountain, going on a cruise, or grabbing a nap.

I look at leisure as "time off" from my normal routine. Russell Tynes calls it a relief from hard work and observed that, "Wasting time is negative, but there is something positive about idleness. . . . Idleness is a . . . commitment to relaxation."[3]

Some people mistakenly believe that anytime we're idle or resting, we're wasting time, but Scripture advises us to rest. Jesus acknowledged the importance of leisure by offering to help us rest. He said, "Come to Me, all who are weary and heavy laden, and I will give you rest" (Matt. 11:28).

Don Herold attributes this misconception about the difference between wasting time and leisure to the frantic activity in our fast-paced society. He observes: "If today's average American is confronted with an hour of leisure, he is likely to palpitate with panic. An hour with nothing to do? He jumps into a car and drives off fiercely in pursuit of diversion. We 'catch' a train, 'grab' a bit of lunch. Everything has to be active and electric. We need less leg action, and more acute observation, as we go. Slow down the muscle and stir up the mind."[4] His point is well taken. Leisure time is vital to our physical and mental health. It is a good-and-necessary thing.

A large portion of life ministry comes under the good-and-necessary category, which includes offering to drive the car pool when it's not your turn because your neighbor overslept, visiting a sick friend in the hospital, teaching a Sunday school class, offering your home to the high school department for their weekly Tuesday night Bible study, making cookies for the bake sale and so on. The list is as limitless as the moving of the Spirit in your life.

This category also caters to our wants. Life would be a

long, tedious string of tasks if we did only what needs to be done and never allow ourselves to do things we want to do simply because we want to do them. I recently met a woman who, at fifty-three, had begun graduate school after raising her family. She hadn't entered a classroom for over twenty years. She told me, "I was scared to death but I wanted to update my skills in my profession. I may never go back to work but I want to do this to expand my horizons." For her at this time, getting an advanced degree is a good-and-necessary thing.

Those Good-but-Unnecessary Items

The fifth category of time-usage is *good-but-unnecessary*. This is the area where we give away time we could keep. Activities in this category are the "good" things we spoke of in the last chapter that distract us, as they did Martha, from God's perfect will for us at any given moment. These activities seem as if they need immediate attention but don't; they seem necessary but aren't. Good-but-unnecessary activities are sometimes things we're trapped into doing, don't want to do, don't like doing, and which, when examined objectively, should be given little, if any, priority.

For example, you say you'll lead your son's scout troop because the man who's organizing it asks you in front of a group of parents. You get roped into teaching a Sunday school class because the superintendent convinces you she can't find anyone else who will do it. You agree to serve on a committee at your child's school because there's a vacancy, they need someone, and they asked you. Leading a scout troop, teaching a Sunday school class, and serving on a school committee are all good things. But they can also mess up your priorities if they're not what God has chosen for you to do. Good-and-unnecessary things consume huge amounts of time you could better redeem elsewhere. They interfere with God's will for how you should redeem your time.

Busy Work

Busy work is the sixth time-usage category. Busy work is work that is somewhat worthwhile but is neither vital nor immediate. Sometimes we use busy work as an excuse for not doing other things. When I don't want to do something, even if it is vital and needs to be done, I can always find something else to do to keep me busy. When I'm having difficulty writing, I can always find some papers to file, phone calls to make, or a floor to mop. Using busy work to fill time we could better use elsewhere or more constructively isn't wise. Using it to relax or as a transition activity when we've finished one thing and aren't ready to go on to the next makes sense. Most projects involve a certain amount of busy work. Writing a book involves typing a manuscript; redecorating a room involves cleaning out closets; making a dress involves buying fabric. Busy work may or may not be constructive, depending on what we're doing and why we're doing it.

You can eliminate most unnecessary busy work by ongoing upkeep. You won't have a lot of filing to do if you process each piece of paperwork or correspondence when you finish with it. You won't have to do windows if you clean one each week, inside and out, as you clean the house. You won't have to clean drawers if you keep them neat.

Some busy work is a way of spending time rather than investing it. It's like blowing money indiscriminately on a shopping spree, and ending up with very little to show for your money, as opposed to investing it so you'll get the best return.

Wasted Time

The seventh time-usage category is *wasted time*. Wasted time is time that could be better spent doing something else. In his book *Getting Things Done,* Edwin C. Bliss says, "Ernest Hemingway is quoted as having defined immoral as 'anything you feel bad after.' I don't know whether that definition will stand up to theological scrutiny, but I do think it can be applied to wasted time."[5]

I think he's right. Most of us sense when we've wasted time, just as we know when we've wasted food. We have been taught and rightfully believe that wasting food is wrong. For example, we've been conditioned to take only as much as we can eat and to clean our plates. We wouldn't fill our plates with food and then scrape it into the garbage without taking a bite (or at least feeding it to the dog). Throwing out perfectly good food is a waste.

Sadly, that is how some people treat time. Every day, God fills our lives with twenty-four precious hours. He grants us 1440 minutes; 86,400 seconds. We frequently waste huge portions of the time He allots us. We discard the minutes and hours like garbage, instead of cautiously consuming every morsel.

No one can tell you how or if you're wasting your time. You have to decide that for yourself. You must determine how to redeem it to the fullest and conserve where conservation is necessary to use it in the most economical way. That is accomplished by centering your activities in vital, immediate, and good-and-necessary categories.

People who focus on busy work and good-but-unnecessary activities, waste an inordinate amount of time. They fail to distinguish between the important and unimportant, the urgent and vital because they generally use one of three inappropriate methods to decide what to do and when to do it: They rely on habit, circumstances, or impulse.

DECIDING HOW TO USE YOUR TIME

Relying on habit is a good way to manage time *if* our time-usage habits are constructive, but "I've always done it this way" is a poor reason for deciding to do something. Performing strictly out of habit runs us off the road of progress into the rut of routine, locks us into one way of doing things—the way we've always done them—and keeps us from exploring new possibilities about how to invest our time. Some habits stifle creativity, dull efficiency, and consume our time unnecessarily. For example, if you changed your habits could you find simpler, more time-efficient ways to organize your paperwork, handle your phone calls, to run errands, or to cook dinner?

Responding to Circumstances

You can see how relying totally on habit is a poor way to decide how to use your time. So is responding to circumstances, although it's the method many people use. They do whatever is placed in front of them at any given moment. They do not make thoughtful, intelligent, time-usage decisions; they respond to their circumstances and consequently are at the mercy of their environment. They're easy to recognize: the homemaker who waits until her house is filthy to clean it, the neighbor who waits until the car breaks down to get it fixed, the man who waits until his wardrobe is a disaster to buy clothes, the woman who participates on a committee because she is assigned a position, or the student who goofs off all semester and has to cram at the last minute to pass a course. Responding to circumstances usually is a monumental waste of time.

Following Your Impulses

Following one's impulses is also an inappropriate determiner of time usage. Some people live their lives doing whatever they feel like doing whenever they feel like doing it. There's certainly nothing wrong with spontaneity; it adds an air of excitement to life and offers an occasional break in routine. An unexpected change of plans is fun and refreshing but extemporaneous, impetuous activity quickly wears thin as an ongoing lifestyle. People who perform by impulse don't redeem time; they squander it.

People who consistently perform out of habit, whether in response to circumstances or on impulse, create time problems because they ignore some basic time-management principles. Ignoring them doesn't keep them from functioning any more than jumping off a roof negates the law of gravity. Time ecologists, people who want to manage their time successfully, take advantage of time-management principles and incorporate them into their daily routines.

TIME-MANAGEMENT PRINCIPLES

We've already explored three scriptural tenets. We discovered, in the third chapter of Ecclesiastes, that there is an appropriate, appointed time to do everything. Christ's lesson to Martha established that there is only one thing God wants us doing at any given moment. In Paul's letter to the Ephesians, we learned that God expects us to redeem our time. Now let's look at four secular principles.

Here's one we've all heard often: *You can always find the time if you want to do something badly enough.* Desire motivates. Generally speaking, most of us find a way to do exactly what we want to do. If you honestly want to manage your time well, you'll find a way to do it.

I'm always amused that my friend Vera can find time to shop for clothes, to go out to lunch, to talk on the phone for an hour but never has enough time to clean her house properly, do the laundry, or get dinner on the table on time. You can learn to manage time properly if you want to badly enough. If you don't, it's not because you can't but because you aren't willing to give up certain activities, break some bad habits, or restructure your priorities and categorize time correctly.

The next principle is: *Time-management depends on the kind of person you are, not on what you do.* You can't permanently restructure your performance by reorganizing minor, inconsequential activities any more than you can restructure the floor plan of a house by rearranging the furniture. Basic time-management problems are merely the symptom of an undisciplined lifestyle. If you want to manage your time well, you have to change your thinking. Deprogram bad time-usage habits and discipline yourself to use time properly, not merely shuffle around activities.

Professor C. Northcote Parkinson devised the next time-management principle: *Work expands to fill time available for its completion.* This means if you decide a job will take four hours to complete, it will. So if you make less time available for a specific task, you will get it done more quickly.

For instance, if you decide weeding the lawn is going to take all morning, chances are it will. But you could probably save time if you plan to do it in two hours.

Employing Parkinson's Law helps us conserve minutes and seconds, which add up to hours that accumulate into days. Following these five steps will help you use this principle to your advantage.

1. Time how long it takes you to do certain tasks, especially those that consume large portions of your time. Don't rush or try to beat the clock, just go at your normal pace. Record how much time you spend weeding the garden, writing out checks for the bills, vacuuming the family room, talking on the phone during any twenty-four hours, or whatever.

2. Determine if there is a way to do each job more efficiently. Are there any steps you could eliminate or procedures you could simplify?

3. Decide on a suitable but shorter length of time to do each task. Think in *seconds,* not minutes.

4. After you've decided on a time frame, the next time you do the job, set a timer and race the clock.

5. If you overextended the new time estimation, determine why the task took as long as it did and try again. By using Parkinson's Law, eventually you will be able to whittle a good number of seconds and minutes from almost everything you do.

The next time-management principle is the brainchild of Italian economist-sociologist Velfredo Pareto. It states: *The significant items in a given group normally constitute a relatively small portion of the total items in a group.* I know. That sounded like Italian to me too the first time I read it, but it *is* translatable. Pareto's Law is also called the "80/20 Rule." Simplified, it means if you arrange everything you do in order of value and productivity, 80% of what you accomplish would result from 20% of what you do. For example, 80% of the dirt in your home is in the most used 20% of the house; 80% of the work in a church is done by 20% of the members; 80% of the information you need is contained in 20% of the papers you shuffle; 80% of the useful knowledge you gain comes from 20% of what you hear and read; and 80% of your "remaining fruit" comes from 20% of your ministry.

Consequently, on any list of ten priorities, two will produce the best, most valuable results. In other words, 20% of the things you do produce 80% of the benefits, so "it's important to remind yourself again and again not to get bogged down on low-value activities but to focus on the 20% where the value is."[6]

Edwin Bliss explains that "The Pareto Principle can be of great help in coping with a long list of tasks. . . . It helps to know that most of the benefit to be derived from doing what is on the list is related to just two or three items. *Select those two or three, allocate a block of time to work on each of them, and concentrate on getting them done.*"[7]

Categorizing time usage and applying time-management principles will help us waste less time and consume it more carefully by distributing it wisely and compressing every moment. "So waste no time on fruitless quests, that get you nowhere in the end. The gold of time is yours to squander, or with care, to use and spend" (Patience Strong, source unknown).

WORKSHOP

I. After each statement, write whether you strongly agree, agree, have no opinion, disagree, or strongly disagree with what it says. Then, write one sentence under each telling *why* you answered as you did. What do your answers tell you about your attitude toward time usage?

   1. I have a right to have time to myself, to be alone to do things I enjoy.

   2. Work and leisure activities are equally enjoyable.

   3. It's best to put off until the last minute something I dislike doing.

   4. Schedules ruin the spontaneity and fun of life and should be kept to a minimum.

   5. Watching television is wasting time.

   6. Taking an afternoon nap when I'm not ill or haven't lost sleep at night is wasting time.

   7. I am frequently bored because I do not have enough to do.

   8. I am frequently frustrated because I don't have enough time to do everything I'm supposed to do.

9. I resent taking time to do things I don't like or want to do.

II. Doing a time-usage survey will help you determine how you use your time. Under the appropriate heading, list as many activities as you can that you've done during the past week.

1. *Vital*

2. *Emergency*

3. *Good-but-unnecessary*

4. *Wasted time*

5. *Immediate*

6. *Good-and-necessary*

7. *Busy work*

Write a paragraph describing what this survey reveals about the way you use your time. List five specific steps you can (and hopefully will) take to increase involvement in the vital and good-and-necessary categories.

III. List ten time-use decisions you made this past week. Put "H" by the ones you performed out of habit, "C" by the ones where you responded to circumstances, "S" by spur-of-the-moment decisions, and "P" by the ones you planned and prioritized. What do your answers reveal about the methods you use when making time-usage decisions? How can you improve the way you make such decisions?

Chapter Twelve

REDEEMING YOUR TIME INSTEAD OF GIVING IT AWAY

"A wise heart knows the proper time and procedure" (Ecclesiastes 8:5).

Knowing proper procedures is essential to success. Without formats and instructions, we wouldn't know what to do, how to do it, or when to do it. I learned how to operate my food processor, which looked very complicated to use, by reading the instruction book; I learned how to use my camera by following the procedures outlined by the manufacturer. Procedures help us put knowledge into practice.

Now that we've learned some time-management principles, let's explore some specific ways to implement them. Ecclesiastes 8:5 says, "A wise heart knows the proper time and procedure." Walking wisely depends on knowing proper time-management procedures. Following them guarantees we'll be better equipped to redeem our time, instead of thoughtlessly giving it away.

BECOME MORE AWARE OF TIME

First, *become more aware of time.* Most people believe that time management begins with task management, restructuring what they do; however, time management really starts with *time,* not activities. To manage your time effectively, you must begin by analyzing how you use and misuse your time before you can take steps to correct it.

Some people find that keeping a time diary is helpful. It doesn't have to be anything elaborate. A small notebook to record every task you do throughout the day and the time each task consumes is adequate. You may think that this kind of detailed accountability is unnecessary, but keeping a journal can create a renewed awareness of how you approach and use time. For example, Angie discovered she was spending six hours a day watching television. That's 2190 hours a year, 131,400 minutes, or 7,884,000 seconds! Are you aware of how much time you consume watching television or talking on the telephone or running errands? You should be. Start thinking in terms of time. Become aware of it as a consumable, perishable, irreplaceable natural resource in your life. Don't make any changes at first; just take notice of how you use the *minutes* and *seconds*.

IDENTIFY AND PLUG TIME LEAKS

The second procedure for managing time is to *identify and plug time leaks*. Time leaks are the minutes and seconds we inadvertently let slip from our lives. Right now, my car has a gas leak. It's so tiny I can't find it, but I can smell it. I realize it's been there for several weeks because my car has progressively been consuming more gasoline for no apparent reason. So, tomorrow I'm taking it in for repairs. Time leaks are like that gas leak. They are difficult to locate and so small they almost seem irrelevant; however, if they aren't traced and stopped, they are costly.

Here are a few common time leaks. (You'll notice that several of them are good-but-unnecessary items.) Socializing indiscriminately, especially on the telephone, is a predominant one.

Self-indulgence is another: devoting too many hours to leisure activities, going on too many shopping trips, lunching too often with friends, or taking too many naps. One of my friends spends forty-five minutes every morning putting on her make-up. I don't take that long to shower, shampoo and dry my hair, do my make-up, get dressed, and go out the door.

Overkill, insisting that every little detail be done perfectly according to your own standards, destroys schedules and lets time escape undetected. When my kids were young, they never made their beds as neatly as I made mine. I could have made them over myself, but I settled for the bedspread being on the bed and covering the pillow because it saved me time, as well as maintained their dignity.

Do-it-yourself projects, as homey and creative as they sound, can create costly time leaks. Sometimes doing it yourself is a good-and-necessary priority; sometimes it isn't. Each of us has to evaluate whether a do-it-yourself project is worth the time it requires. Perhaps it's consuming time that we could better spend elsewhere. Take sewing as an example. I used to make almost all of my clothes, and when my daughters were young, I made theirs. The money I saved was well worth the time I spent. Several years ago, I had to stop making my clothes because I could no longer afford the time. I can't maintain a full-time career as a mother, wife, homemaker, writer and speaker and design and make my own wardrobe.

Some common do-it-yourself time leaks people often mention are baking bread instead of buying it, washing the car instead of taking it to a car wash, doing math by hand instead of using a calculator, and doing taxes, yard work, or perhaps, housecleaning when you could afford to hire them done and need the time more than the money.

Another common time leak is watching television for no reason; merely turning on the set and *then* consulting the directory to see what's on, instead of sitting down to watch a specific program. Some others are line drying clothes instead of using a clothes dryer, ironing no-iron items, cooking single batches of anything that will freeze, shopping too often, writing or going somewhere instead of phoning if a phone call would accomplish the same purpose.

Idling, the gaps of inactivity that occur within certain tasks, is another source of time leakage. Commuting, waiting in a doctor's office, stopping at red lights, or standing in the back of a line are idle time. For example, to buy groceries, you have to spend ten minutes in the car to get to the store because of stopping at red lights and stop signs along the way. To do your banking, you usually wait in line for a few minutes, too. We don't create idle time, it's just there.

DON'T JUST IDLE—DO SOMETHING

Most people waste idle time; however, using it is like finding an extra hour or two every week. For example, the last time I went to the doctor for my yearly physical, I took stationery and a crossword puzzle book. I've learned from experience that obstetricians seldom run on schedule. Although I had the first appointment after lunch, I still phoned the office at 11:45 to see if they were running on time. They were then, but when I got there at 2:00, the nurse informed me that the doctor had been detained at the hospital for a delivery and would be forty-five minutes late.

I didn't mind because I'd come prepared to use that idle time. The woman who had the appointment after mine was a nervous wreck. She flipped through several magazines, kept asking the nurse if the doctor was on his way, went out into the hall several times to smoke a cigarette, paced the floor, and kept looking at her watch. Finally, she said to me, "This is such a waste of time." Then, she looked at the stack of correspondence I was wading through and said, "I bet you're glad you brought something to do." I certainly was.

Plugging Time Leaks

Taking something to do whenever you go somewhere, especially if you know you might have to wait, is a good way to plug time leaks and make the most of idle time. It's a good way to catch up on a lot of little things you can't seem to work into your schedule, like writing thank-you notes, hemming a skirt, reading a magazine article, or planning your weekly menu. I always carry a steno pad, crossword puzzle book, and pen in my purse, just in case.

There are numerous other things we can do to plug time leaks. One is to be aware of when and where they occur. Another is to plan ways to use idle time. When you're commuting, think, pray, listen to tapes, plan your day, think through problems, or plan a project.

Another way to plug time leaks is to eliminate as much idle time as possible. Make definite appointments whenever you can. Call ahead when you have an appointment to confirm whether you need to be there on time. I gained half an hour last week by phoning my hairdresser to see if he was running on schedule; he wasn't. Do errands when you're on your way somewhere, instead of making special trips. Choose the best time to go somewhere when there will be fewer people and less congestion.

Carrie used her entire lunch hour on Friday going to the bank, about a ten-minute drive from her office. When she realized this was a wasteful time leak, she moved her account to a bank in the building where she works and now banks during her afternoon coffee break.

Consolidate Time

Consolidating time also helps plug time leaks. Some things we do demand our full attention; others don't. Doing two or more lesser tasks at a time is a good way to compress minutes and hours. I make most of my phone calls in the morning when I'm cleaning the kitchen or when I'm folding laundry. I bake cookies and do laundry while I'm cleaning the family room. I do mending and write letters while I'm watching television. Remember, minutes add up to hours, which add up to days.

THINK SMALL

A third time-redeeming procedure is to *divide large jobs into manageable time segments.* The key to successful time management is to think small. Many tasks seem absolutely impossible when we approach them as one big unit, so we put them off or don't do them at all. They shrink considerably when we break them into manageable segments.

That is certainly true of writing a book. Sitting down to write five hundred or more pages seems overwhelming, but it isn't nearly so ominous when I outline the book first. I begin by writing one paragraph describing each chapter. Next, I construct a one-page outline of each chapter, then outline each section in every chapter in detail. Finally, I fill in the outline with words. Gradually, by breaking that big task into less complex parts, paragraphs become sections, which become chapters, which become a book.

Thinking big about how to use time is self-defeating because you focus on hours and days, not the minutes and seconds that you need to conserve. Instead of thinking you have to clean the entire house, focus on one room at a time and subdivide the duties. If you're going to clean the bedroom, say to yourself, *I'll dust the dresser in ten seconds, the bedframe in ten seconds, the chest of drawers in thirty seconds, the nightstand in thirty seconds. I'll change the bed in five minutes, clean the mirror in one minute, dust-vacuum the drapes in four minutes, and vacuum the room in three.* Using this approach, you'll clean your bedroom in fourteen minutes.

Dr. Robert C. Riley, a professor at the University of Cincinnati, said, "You can eat an elephant if you do it one bite at a time." Dividing large jobs into manageable time segments helps you "eat the elephant" of overwhelming tasks.

LET SOMEONE ELSE DO IT

A fourth time-saving procedure is to *learn to delegate*. Many of us waste time doing things someone else could or should be doing. We need to learn to delegate. There are various reasons why we don't. Some of us suffer from the "if I don't do it, no one will" syndrome; others the "no one can do it as well as I" attitude. Thinking we're indispensable is actually a form of pride and encourages us to waste a great deal of time.

Some people don't delegate because they fear they can't relinquish responsibility without giving up authority: They feel insecure if not in total control. Others don't delegate because they're more concerned with process—*how* something is done—than with results: They want things done their way or not at all. And some people don't delegate because they don't know how: They know they're suffering from time overload but don't know how to start releasing responsibility to others.

Suggestions for Delegating

Each of us needs to develop a workable system for delegating. Here are six suggestions to get you going. First, *accept that you must delegate*. Paul stressed the importance of division of labor. When the Corinthian Christians were choosing up sides over which teacher God had sent, he said, "The Lord gave opportunity to each one. I planted, Apollos watered, but God was causing the growth (1 Cor. 3:5–6).

Jethro, the father-in-law of Moses, had some wise counsel for his son-in-law about delegating: "When Moses' father-in-law saw all that he was doing for the people he said, 'What is this thing that you are doing for the people? Why do you alone sit as judge and all the people stand about you from morning until evening?'" (Exod. 18:14).

Moses had a very noble reason for not delegating: "Because the people come to me to inquire of God. When they have a dispute, it comes to me, and I judge between a man and his neighbor, and make known the statutes of God and His laws" (Exod. 18:15–16).

But Jethro didn't commend Moses for being so involved in his ministry. Instead, he rebuked him for not delegating some of his duties: "The thing that you are doing is not good. You will surely wear out . . . for the task is too heavy for you; you cannot do it alone" (Exod. 18:17–18). No one can do it alone—whether running a church, maintaining a household, or administrating a corporation—everyone needs to delegate.

Second, *delegate things you don't have the aptitude to do or can't do.* Trying to perform where you have little talent wastes a great amount of time. Don't use ignorance as an excuse but admit that everyone, including you, has limitations. Then, delegate to supplement your lacks.

Third, *decide what you're doing that someone else could or should be doing.* If you don't delegate, you do work and accept responsibility that isn't yours. The apostle Paul, who was a master at delegating, operated on this premise: "Each one shall bear his own load" (Gal. 6:5). That principle applies regardless of a person's age or sex. Delegating helps others learn basic skills, such as doing the laundry or cooking, and develop their talents, as well as free up your time.

Fourth, *learn to ask for help.* This is especially important for those of you who seem so efficient that nobody realizes how burdensome your time loads are. There are two ways to ask for help. One is a silent, indirect approach; let the job show the need. If your daughter complains because her favorite blouse, which she wore two days ago, isn't clean, you say, "I don't have time to do laundry every day. Why don't you gather a load of colored clothes from the hamper right now and wash them with your blouse?" What doesn't get done will help people realize that you've been doing more than you should.

Letting the job show the need means cutting back on the *quantity* of work you do, but it doesn't have to diminish the quality. Actually, if you spread yourself less thin, you'll probably do a better job. Cutting back is an effective way to ask for help.

Another method is to use the direct approach. Remember, people aren't mind readers. They don't know what we need unless we ask, but many times we don't because doing so seems to be a sign of weakness. And, haven't we all been conditioned to believe we should perform like supermen or superwomen?

If you need help, ask for it. If you don't have time to cook dinner *and* vacuum the carpet, put your pride aside and ask someone to do it for you. If you'd have to spend three hours at home typing the report you spent all day preparing because the boss wants it tomorrow, let him know you'll have time to write it but not to type it. Saying you need help is an effective way to delegate duties.

Be Considerate

A necessity when you delegate is to be considerate. Don't dump all of the "dirty work" onto others and save the best or easiest jobs for yourself. Try to assign tasks that relate to a person's interests and talents whenever possible and rotate the less pleasant ones. When you ask someone to do something, make certain he knows exactly what needs to be done and how to do it. Don't assume he does. Be willing to take time to show someone how to do something.

A final suggestion about delegating is that it has to be done with no strings attached, except that a job be done decently and on time. Don't impose your methods on another person. When I cook, I put away everything and do dishes as I go. My daughter Cathy cooks an entire meal then cleans up, but we both manage to get dinner on the table.

DON'T GIVE TIME AWAY

A fifth procedure for managing time and plugging leaks is *don't give away time you can keep*. Don't let superfluous events or people who don't matter to you steal your time. Have you ever noticed how many "Dear Abby" letters are about friends or neighbors who drop in at all hours, phone incessantly, or expect someone to be at their disposal?

Some people drain us physically and emotionally and make unreasonable demands on our time. They work against God's will for our lives, so we have to eliminate their influence. I know that sounds contrary to the Christian ethic, but even Paul was buffeted by a messenger of Satan. Some theologians theorize that the messenger was a person who followed Paul, interfered with his ministry, criticized him unfairly, and made unreasonable demands on his time.

Remember, there is only one thing God wants you doing at any given moment. *You can't minister to every person who crosses your path.* Redeeming the time means investing it in the people and circumstances the Lord has reserved for you.

Making such choices isn't simple. People are always asking me to look over manuscripts they're writing. I was taking hours every month to answer letters from strangers or acquaintances who became my "good friends" after I'd met them once. I was frustrated, but at the same time, I felt an obligation because the Lord has given me a writing ministry. So, I'd answer each letter in detail, sometimes three or four pages. It reached a point where I was spending as much time answering requests about how to write a book as I was writing my own. I knew I had to do something because I felt used. So I made a brief outline of suggestions I could send to those people, along with a list of editors they could contact. I realized that I was giving away time I could keep by getting involved in something good-but-unnecessary, for me.

Telephone Temptation

Another way we give away time we could keep is by talking on the telephone. Every time-management expert I've read or heard lecture mentions this problem. Dr. Dru Scott notes, "The telephone intrudes on privacy, interrupts work, ruins repose. People often tell me that they could manage their time wonderfully well if it weren't for the telephone. If you consistently mismanage your telephone time, there's no doubt it can be a tyrant. But used to your advantage, it's a wonderfully helpful tool. It's up to you."[1]

There are several things you can do to keep from giving away time on the telephone. Don't let callers intrude into your home and space. You aren't obligated to talk to every solicitor or survey taker who phones any more than you have to let every salesperson who knocks on your door walk into your home. Talk only when and if you want or need to talk.

I have a policy not to talk to any salesperson I haven't contacted. When one phones, I don't even answer their "How are you today?" I simply say I do not take unsolicited sales calls and hang up. No, that isn't rude; usurping someone's time, even via the telephone, is.

Don't socialize on the phone unless there's no other way. It's a convenient way to keep in touch but isn't as suitable as personal contact. It's easy to misinterpret meanings and reactions when there's no eye-to-eye contact. Think of the telephone as an instrument of communication rather than a place to have a conversation.

Don't let telephone calls be a priority. You don't have to answer the phone just because it rings nor talk just because you answer it. Make it a rule not to let the telephone interfere with your work and don't use it unless you have time. If someone phones when you're busy, don't get sidetracked by a conversation. Make an appointment or set a time to call back when you can concentrate on the call and the caller.

TAKE TIME ALONE

The seventh time-saving procedure is to *take time alone.* Christ did. Matthew 14:23 says He sent the multitudes away and went up to the mountain alone to pray. John records that when the people came to "take Him by force, to make Him king, [He] withdrew again to the mountain by Himself alone" (6:15). The Lord spent time alone when He needed to pray, meditate, or get away from the stress and strife of everyday life. We need to follow His example and retreat and refuel, so we can productively redeem our time.

Spending time alone gives us a chance to get in touch with our innermost thoughts and feelings and refresh both our souls and our bodies. It's easier to concentrate, plan, evaluate, and just relax when you're alone and there's no one to make any demands on your time. It's my opinion that everyone—adult or child—should spend some time alone every day, so we can learn to live comfortably with ourselves.

DON'T TRY TO DO TOO MUCH IN TOO LITTLE TIME

The eighth time-management procedure is *allow yourself time.* The old adage "haste makes waste" is true. G. K. Chesterton observed that, "One of the great disadvantages of hurry is that it takes such a long time." When we hurry, we make mistakes that claim more time than if we hadn't rushed. Trying to do too much in too little time is counterproductive because it decreases our efficiency and enjoyment. I can't count the number of times I've spilled something in the kitchen when I was rushing to fix dinner or when I've forgotten something as I hurried out of the house and had to go back for it.

Don't keep such a tight schedule that you're always pressed for time. Don't think you have to be busy every minute of the day. Cramming your schedule with activity isn't redeeming time, it's gulping it down. Life should be savored, like each tantalizing bit of a gourmet meal.

Syndicated columnist Ellen Goodman observed, "There are times when we all end up completing a day or week or a month as if it were a task to be crossed off the list with a sigh. In the effort to make it all work, it can become all work. We become one-minute managers, mothers, husbands. We end up spending our time on the fly."[2] That's the world's way, not God's way. Relaxing, having fun, taking time to stop and smell the roses are good-and-necessary time expenditures.

MAKE THE MOST OF YOUR MOODS

A ninth way to redeem time is to *make the most of your moods*. Most of us have preset times when we do things and are very dependent on our clocks and watches. In many cases, we'd do better to respond to our unique, God-created body rhythms. It makes sense to do the difficult jobs when we feel most energetic, the thought-demanding ones when we're most mentally alert, and the easy ones when we're running out of steam. And, it makes sense to get up and do something when we can't sleep.

My friend Sharon is definitely a night person. She functions poorly before 10 A.M. and doesn't come alive until after lunch. She's a great asset in her office because by midafternoon, when everyone else is running down, she's at the peak of performance. She handles a lot of business that would otherwise get pushed aside until the next day. She and her co-workers know how to make the most of her moods.

FINISH WHAT YOU START

The tenth time-redeeming procedure is *finish what you start before you move on to something else*. Or, if you're doing a big job, finish a specific portion of it. Don't start to clean the closet and then stop when you've piled all of the clothes on the bed to weed the lawn. Don't go to the store to buy a wedding present and shop for a dress. Don't start figuring your taxes but forget to come back to finish them when you go to the kitchen to fix a cup of coffee. Leaving a job undone is a form of procrastination.

Fragmented activity wastes time. In his book *Success,* Michael Korda advises, "When you set out to do something, *complete it.* Energy thrives on achievement and declines as things drag on."[3] Sticking with something once it's started creates momentum and helps you work efficiently at a steady pace. I don't have to tell you what being interrupted does to concentration. Having to answer the phone or the door or stop in the middle of a project when the creative juices are flowing are all monumental distractions. Once you've prioritized a task and committed yourself to it, sticking with it saves time and frustration.

LEARN TO SAY NO

The eleventh and final time-redeeming suggestion is to *learn to say no.* Willard S. Krabill, M.D., said, "Those who are mentally and emotionally healthy are those who have learned to say Yes, when to say No, and when to say Whoopee!" Edwin C. Bliss, author of *Getting Things Done,* said, "Of all the time saving techniques ever developed the most effective is the use of the word no."[4]

First, we have to learn to say no to ourselves: "No, I won't stop until I've finished this job," "No, I won't waste time talking on the telephone," "No, I won't do something until I've thought about and prioritized it," "No, I won't try to do it all by myself or perfectly," "No, I won't put off doing this no matter how badly I want to."

We also have to learn to say no to others, which is difficult because from childhood we've been taught that saying no is impolite and selfish. Mommy tells Tommy it's time to go to bed. He says no because he wants to stay up. Mommy says, "Don't tell me no. That's not nice." Your teenage daughter's English teacher asks her to play the lead in the school play. She declines and her grade suffers.

We waste a lot of time because we don't say no often enough or we say yes too readily. Saying no is not rude or selfish if a "no" will help us follow the Lord's injunction to redeem the time. Christ said no to many things: people who were insincere and tried to distract Him from His mission, temporal situations that had no eternal value, and religious activities.

There are numerous other reasons why we don't say no. We feel sorry for the person who asks us to do something. We feel responsible to solve others' time problems by saying yes. The person making the request intimidates us, makes us feel guilty, or asks us at a time when saying no would put us in a bad light. Maybe we want to be liked and accepted and win someone's favor so we say yes. Perhaps we're flattered at being asked to say yes because it's a feather in our cap. Mainly most of us say yes, even when we don't want to, because we don't know how to say no. We need to learn. Saying no can make us more competent servants of the Lord and be an extremely effective way to redeem time.

WORKSHOP

I. The following quiz should help you assess whether you're redeeming your time or giving it away. Fill in the appropriate answer on the line provided (never, seldom, sometimes, frequently, always).

1. I am self-indulgent with my time. _____
2. People complain because I take too long getting ready. _____
3. I am a "stickler" for details. _____
4. When someone helps me with a job, I insist he does it my way. _____
5. I watch at least two hours of television every day. _____
6. I focus more on hours and days than on minutes and seconds. _____
7. I prefer doing things myself to involving others and relinquishing responsibility. _____
8. I socialize on the telephone an hour or more every day. _____
9. I'm too busy to spend time alone. _____
10. I feel guilty when I take time for myself. _____
11. I'm always running late. _____
12. I live by the clock. _____
13. I'm involved in at least five major projects at any given time. _____
14. I have difficulty finishing a job once I start it. _____
15. I say yes without thinking. _____

Now tally your score. Give yourself 1 point for each never, 2 for each seldom, 3 for each sometimes, 4 for each frequently, and 5 for each always.

If your score was 15–25, you win the Time Redemption of the Year Award. You're probably a perfectionist and somewhat inflexible about the way you use your time. You need to loosen up a bit because you're too preoccupied with time and more concerned with the process than with results.

If your score was 26–40, you have a balanced perspective about time and are an expert at redeeming it. Keep up the good work!

If your score was 41–60, you use your time well in some areas but mismanage it in others. You waste or give away about half of your time. You need to work at pinpointing your personal time problems and take specific steps to eliminate them.

If your score was 61–75, please turn to the start of this book and read it again, carefully. You need to start managing your time. Don't procrastinate! Do it now.

II. On the chart below, list five common time leaks in your life. Then, write a sentence telling what you can do to plug each of the leaks.

Time Leak	Plug
1.	
2.	
3.	
4.	
5.	

III. Think of a major project you did recently or are going to be doing in the near future. Break it into manageable segments. Outline activities you'll need to do in each segment and how long each task should take, in minutes or seconds. (No hours please.)

IV. In the space below, list twenty-five jobs you do. Put an "X" by those you could delegate. Put a "*" by those you should delegate because you know someone could do them better. Put an "H" by the ones where you need to ask for help.

V. Are you giving away time you could keep? Name one person who consistently and unnecessarily infringes on your time. Write a paragraph explaining what you can do to remedy this situation.

Chapter Thirteen   THAT "DIRTY" WORD NO

"Say just a simple 'Yes, I will' or 'No, I won't' " (Matthew 5:37 LB).

I knew why she was calling the moment she said she was Mrs. Jones from a certain charity. Someone from that organization has phoned me every spring for the last eight years to ask if I'd collect for their door-to-door fund drive in my neighborhood. I'd always said yes before. I admire the organization and its work, I felt it was a way to serve the Lord in my community, and I know how difficult getting someone to donate two or three hours can be. But this year, I had equally valid reasons for saying no. I was having out-of-town guests during collection week, my desk was piled with work, I thought it was time someone else did their share, and I simply did not want to.

Mrs. Jones was quite shocked when I told her I wouldn't be able to collect this year. She was not willing to take no for an answer. Our conversation went something like this:

"But you've collected for us for the past eight years."

"I know."

"We're only asking for a couple of hours of your time."

"I know, but I won't collect this year."

"You do such a fine job, Mrs. Berry. You always get your money in on time. We hate to lose you. We do so appreciate your help."

I thanked her and told her I was certain she could find someone who was equally as competent.

"Mrs. Berry," she persisted, "I'm sure you understand

how much we rely on regulars like you. It saves us time and money."

"I do understand," I assured her, "but I think it's time to give someone else a chance to support your organization in this way."

I could tell Mrs. Jones was getting angry by the tone of her voice, but she didn't stop. "I assumed *you* were supportive of the organization, since you've helped in the past."

"I am," I affirmed, "but I can't collect this year."

Next, she recounted the goals of the organization and reminded me of its fine work. I assured her I'd make a cash donation, as usual, but that I wouldn't collect.

"We're really not asking much," she replied.

"I know, but I still have to decline."

"Well," she huffed, "I think you'd feel a bit selfish turning us down when we're asking for so little to help so many. Your refusal means I'll have to call around to find a volunteer to replace you."

When I didn't say anything, she asked if I'd be willing to collect if she couldn't find anyone to take my place to which I firmly replied, "No, not this year."

Next she tried the pity routine. "Well, I don't know what I'm going to do," she said softly. I suggested she phone a retirement home in the area to see if she couldn't enlist some senior citizens who have time on their hands.

Eventually, she finally realized the irresistible force had met the immovable object, so she thanked me for my time and hung up.

You've probably been in similar situations, where someone did everything in her power to manipulate you into saying yes. Look at the techniques Mrs. Jones used: flattery (I do such a good job), guilt (my saying no would cost the organization time and money and cause her problems), coercion (she appealed to my sense of compassion—how could I *not* help this group), and criticism (I was being selfish). There was a time when she could have worn me down, but that was before I learned the value and necessity of saying no and how to do it without feeling defensive, upset, or guilty. That's something we all need to learn if we're going to manage our time well. Let's look at some pointers that will help us become skillful at saying no without making it sound like a "dirty" word.

BREAK THE YES HABIT

First, we need to *break the yes habit*. Most of us say yes out of habit; we've been conditioned. We're flattered at being chosen; we start thinking we're indispensable. Saying yes is easier and more comfortable than saying no. We never risk rejection with a yes because no one ever gets angry at us for responding positively to a request.

People know "yessers" and take full advantage of them. A young woman I know is generous to a fault. She's always the one who brings refreshments, does the typing, and buys the materials for the weekly Bible study she attends. Recently, she had a serious financial setback, so she had to stop doing all of those things because she simply didn't have the money. Her withdrawal was a blessing in disguise. She realized how much time she was devoting, how much money she was spending (baking goodies for twenty-five or more people every week isn't cheap), and how she, and everyone else, took her service for granted. She was ministering out of habit without evaluating whether she was following the leading of the Spirit.

THE "PIC" PLAN

Applying one basic rule can help break the yes habit: *never say yes without thinking.* Whenever you're asked to do anything, never respond immediately. Always wait until some time has lapsed. I developed a formula I call the "Pic Plan":

Prioritize, **I**nvestigate and **C**onsult. When I'm asked to do something, I first *pray* about whether I should say yes or no. I ask the Lord to help me discern His will for me at that moment. Second, I *prioritize* the request and decide if it is a vital or good-and-necessary way for me to use my time. Third, I *consult* my calendar to see if the task I've been asked to do will conflict with any existing plans. Fourth, I *investigate* the cost in time, effort, and goals that saying yes will involve. Some things that sound like magnificent opportunities when I'm asked to do them end up being horrendous, time-devouring undertakings in the cold light of reality. Sometimes, something that seems simple on the surface isn't and ends up consuming vast, unexpected amounts of time, as well as emotional and physical energy.

That happened to me several years ago. I was asked to be the Bible study chairperson for a Christian women's service auxiliary. I'd taught in the organization and knew how it operated. The job, as described to me, was tailor-made to my talents and seemed simple enough: help select study materials and recruit, train, and monitor the teachers who taught at the monthly chapter meetings.

After I said yes, I discovered I was required to visit each of the twenty-eight chapters once during the year to hear every teacher present a lesson. I also had to attend a monthly board meeting and serve on the curriculum selection committee. I tried to do the job at first but quickly realized that doing it well was going to take more time than I could spare, so I offered my resignation. Rather than letting me quit, the board asked the woman who had filled the position before me to be my assistant. She agreed to visit the chapters, do teacher evaluations, and help recruit. So I stayed, but I was certainly relieved when that year was over.

Evaluate Each Request

Evaluating each request carefully will help break the yes habit. Decide if whatever you're considering will overload you with too much responsibility and if it's something you can do or want to expend time and energy on. I absolutely hate talking on the phone. I always joke that it ranks with going to the dentist or a funeral on my list of favorite things to do. Consequently, I never take any kind of position that involves phoning. When you make a commitment by saying yes, you must be willing to accept responsibility and cope with the time demands that come with the job, gladly and graciously. If you can't, you'd better say no.

Instead of responding on the spot, examine your motives and decide why you're saying yes. Is it because the request stroked your ego? Are you so proud of being asked you can't say no? Is it out of guilt or obligation, even if you aren't obligated? Do you believe you must say yes merely because you've been asked? Do you say yes because you're a genuinely nice person who doesn't want to offend anyone? Maybe you fear rejection or want to be liked. Perhaps you dislike confrontation or don't have confidence in the decisions you make, so you do whatever others ask because you subconsciously assume they know better than you how you should use your time.

Sometimes we say yes to *people* rather than to requests. I do a good many things for my husband, children, and close friends that I wouldn't do for acquaintances or strangers.

Most important, when deciding whether or not to say yes, decide if it's God's specific will for you as an individual. You can't do His bidding by saying yes to everything. Breaking the yes habit is a basic requirement for learning to say no.

I'M TOO BUSY!

Another must is to *make others aware of* your *time demands*. People who ask you to do things usually assume you have the time to do them. Consequently, you need to educate them about what's happening in your life and how you use your time.

Most parents don't know how hard their children work at school and how overwhelming homework can be at times. Very few husbands or wives know how their mates spend their separate time at home or at the office because all they see are results: a paycheck, groceries in the pantry, clean clothes in a closet, a mowed lawn.

For years, George and I have made a habit of giving each other a recap of our day. I've had to take particular care to explain my job to Brian. He used to assume I didn't "work" because I'm self-employed. My office is in my home, and I don't leave the house every day to go to work like his friends' mothers do. I'm here when he comes home from school. I'm available to go to school functions during the day, to serve after-school snacks to the gang, or to run his homework to him if he forgets it. A few years ago, we had a long talk about my being a working mother. I explained to him that all mothers work; I'm busy during the day while he's at school. The house doesn't automatically clean itself, clean laundry doesn't simply appear in the closets, and meals don't cook themselves. I told him I knew he wasn't aware of how much time I spend at my desk working on manuscripts because he didn't see me do these things. Then, I detailed exactly how I spend my days, how I juggle my careers, and how much concentration and research writing requires. He's had a deeper appreciation of my time and position since then.

Educating others about our time demands keeps us from seeming inconsiderate and arbitrary when we say no and helps them think before they ask us to say yes.

RESPECT YOUR TIME

A third necessity for learning to say no is to *respect your own time as much as you respect the time of others.* What you choose to do with your time is as valid as what others decide to do with theirs. It is *more* valid than how any other person thinks you should spend it.

Each of us is accountable to the Lord for the way he uses his time. How embarrassing to stand before Him and say, "Well, I did this because Tom asked, this because Susie told me to, this because Dan made me, this because my children wouldn't, so I had to." We should be able to say, "I did this because I knew, beyond any shadow of doubt, it was Your perfect will for me."

If we automatically say yes, we are letting others— sometimes complete strangers or minor acquaintances— establish our priorities. We're responsible to protect and stick to our personal priorities and to appreciate and use our God-given freedom of choice. We should have enough respect for our time that we don't let others waste it.

DON'T TRY TO BE A SOLVE-IT-ALL

A fourth suggestion that helps us say no is *don't try to solve other people's time problems by saying yes.* You should not assume responsibility for someone else's time problems and expect them to solve yours.

For example, Brian is in a bowling league with three other boys. Last year, two of the mothers had to work on Saturday morning, and the fathers all looked at Saturday as their day off, so guess who ended up driving the kids to the bowling alley almost every week? The other parents would call with one excuse after another and ask if I'd mind driving. They expected me to solve their time problems. When I tried, I ended up with a set of my own.

My reasoning was if I said no, I'd be depriving my son of going bowling. Also, I knew the other boys had no control over what their parents did. I didn't want to penalize them because their parents wouldn't drive. And, driving Brian alone seemed terribly petty, so George and I ended up taking and picking up the team every week. This tied up our Saturday mornings completely.

This year, I told Brian I wasn't going to run a bus service

again. I'd do my share but no more. I explained to him that I understood that the boys' parents have problems driving but that his dad and I have things to do on Saturday mornings, too. So I phoned each parent and set up a car pool, where we drove in alphabetical rotation. We agreed if we couldn't drive, we'd make other arrangements but would not expect anyone in the car pool to be responsible for our driving day.

This worked beautifully for a few weeks. Then Andy's mother phoned and said she wouldn't be able to drive because she had an extra job to do at work and her husband couldn't drive because he was playing golf. In other words, she had a time problem and expected me to solve it for her by saying yes. Consequently, I traded days with her. But the following Saturday when she was supposed to drive, she phoned again. This time her husband's car was being repaired, and she had to take hers to work. I told her I had plans, so she'd have to make other arrangements as we'd agreed we would when we set up the car pool.

Guess what Andy's parents did? (They certainly didn't call any of the other parents in the car pool!) Her husband took her to work, kept the car, and drove the boys to and from the bowling alley. I let them solve their own time problems, and they didn't impose on me again.

Children are masters at passing the buck when it comes to time problems. My friend's son accused her of making him get a failing grade on a report because she hadn't nagged him about finishing it on time. He turned it in late and got an F.

Karen came over one day in tears. Her ten-year-old daughter Vanessa was driving her insane she claimed: "She *will not* get ready for school on time, so she always misses the bus, which means I have to drive her. I lose an hour every morning, not to mention the wear and tear on my nerves. She can't decide what to wear, dawdles over breakfast, and can never find her homework. I hate getting up in the morning because I know I'm going to have to do battle with her."

When I asked Karen what she'd done to try to correct the problem, she said, "Everything! I've talked with her, reasoned with her, explained how she inconveniences me, threatened, spanked, taken away her allowance and television, had Greg talk to her. Nothing works."

She asked if I had any ideas. I recommended that she stop trying to solve Vanessa's time problems and let her child suffer the consequences of her actions. I suggested that she buy Vanessa an alarm clock, tell her that she'd have thirty minutes to get up, dressed, and out to breakfast after it rang. I also suggested that Karen have Vanessa lay out the clothes she was going to wear the next day before she went to bed, that they pick a specific place for Vanessa to put her homework and school books, and that Karen give her one, and only one, fifteen-minute warning in the morning. Most important, I counseled her to tell Vanessa that if she missed the bus, she would have to walk to school or spend the day in her room and take an unexcused absence.

Karen was reluctant. She argued that the school is six miles from their home and that Vanessa is, after all, only ten years old. She'd be making her daughter miss school if she carried through on the plan I suggested. I said, "No, you won't. If she misses, it will be her fault. You'll have done all you should do." I asked her to consider which was more important—a day at school or that Vanessa learn how to manage her time.

A couple of weeks later, Karen phoned. "It worked! It worked!" she squealed. She then excitedly told me how, after talking with her husband, they'd laid down the ground rules and stuck to them. Their ultimatum worked for a couple of days. Then one morning, Vanessa got up late and threw a tantrum when Karen refused to drive her to school. She spent the day in her room. The following morning she was dressed and out to breakfast on time. She hasn't missed the bus since.

Vanessa learned an important lesson and so did Karen:

You can advise and lend a hand, but you can't solve anyone's time problems but your own.

Don't Give in to Criticism

Karen told me that the most difficult thing about standing her ground with her daughter was remaining objective when Vanessa criticized her. Vanessa told Karen she was a mean, selfish mother and she'd never forgive her.

People don't like being told no and may get critical when they are. They take no as a personal rejection, even though that's not our intention, so they retaliate by finding fault with the person who denies their wishes. If we're going to manage our time well, we can't give in to criticism. That's easier said than done. Nobody likes having someone find fault with him, but there are ways to cope with the criticism that is an inevitable response to saying no.

First, don't take the censure personally. People who disapprove of your time-use decisions aren't disapproving of you as a person. They're striking back because you've inconvenienced them or refused to solve their time problems by saying yes. Alan Lakein notes, "Sometimes the way you use your time is bound to make others unhappy. Everybody likes attention. Giving each person the attention he wants takes time. . . . You can never do everything everyone wants—there just isn't time."[1]

Keep your perspective. You aren't doing anything wrong by saying no. Be realistic. Expect some negative reactions. Don't take them personally.

Don't Strike Back

Second, to handle criticism, don't strike back. Criticizing someone who criticizes you usually leads to an argument or at least to an unpleasant confrontation. You don't have to defend yourself to anyone who attacks you unfairly because you gave him an answer he didn't want to hear. In his book *When I Say No, I Feel Guilty,* Dr. Manuel J. Smith states, "In teaching people to cope with manipulative criticism . . . I instruct them *not* to deny the criticism (that's simply responding in kind), not to get defensive, and not to counterattack with criticism of their own"[2] primarily because doing so accomplishes nothing.

Instead, Dr. Smith suggests, "When criticized, you can assertively cope by offering no resistance."[3] He didn't originate that idea. Jesus taught it centuries before: "I say to you, do not resist him who is evil; but whoever slaps you on your right cheek, turn to him the other also" (Matt. 5:39).

This doesn't mean we have to maintain grim-faced, clenched-teeth, stoic silence when someone criticizes us; rather, it means employing what the Proverbs call "a soft answer." Dr. Smith suggests agreeing with truth, agreeing in principle, or agreeing with the odds.

When Mrs. Jones from the charity drive said to me, "But you've collected for us for the past eight years," and "We're only asking for a couple hours of your time," I said, "I know." That's agreeing with truth. A common statement many of you will hear when you start managing your time and saying no is "You've changed" (implying not for the better!). That's true. You can agree. You *have* changed.

Agreeing in principle affirms that you are looking at the situation from the other person's point of view. When Mrs. Jones told me she thought I should feel a bit selfish, I responded by agreeing in principle. I said, "I can see how you would think I'm selfish." I wasn't admitting I *was* selfish or agreeing that I should *feel* selfish but simply saying I understood how she felt.

Agreeing with the odds, according to Dr. Smith, is agreeing "with any possible truth in statements used to criticize us."[4] I agreed with the odds when Mrs. Jones said my refusal would force her to call around to find a replacement for me. She didn't know that would be the case. The next person she called might have said yes, but it could have happened the way she feared. Her statement was a possible truth. I agreed with the odds by letting her know I understood how difficult soliciting volunteer help must be.

The value in this kind of approach is not only that it eliminates arguments and backbiting but also keeps you from defending your time-usage decisions. When you're doing what you think is right, moral, honorable, and God's will for your life, you don't have to defend yourself to anyone.

Don't Feel Guilty

The final necessity for coping with criticism is not to be swayed by criticism. Don't let it undermine your self-confidence or make you feel guilty. In her book *How to Put More Time in Your Life,* Dr. Dru Scott calls guilt the world-champion time waster. She believes it "is implicated in more wasted time and poor time management than any other single emotion."[5]

Most of us automatically feel guilty when we say no because we've been conditioned to believe that saying no is wrong. To most of us, no is a dirty word we associate with failure, weakness, or misconduct. When we use it, we feel guilty. We think we should always say yes because doing so shows we are competent, strong, and morally upright. That is a lie. In many instances, no is affirmative, not negative.

According to Psalm 1, *not* walking in the counsel of the wicked, *not* standing in the path of sinners and *not* sitting in the seat of scoffers are positive steps toward righteousness. A lot of Christians think saying no is a sin. It is not unless we're saying it to the Lord or quenching His Spirit.

Examining the legitimacy of guilt with four simple questions can help us fend off "the guilties." First, what should we feel guilty about? We should feel guilty for stealing valuable time from ourselves and those closest to us by saying yes to peripheral requests. We should feel guilty for wasting time or for saying yes to less than God's best for us as individuals. We should be more bothered by neglecting the vital and good-and-necessary, life-altering activities than we are by saying no.

Second, what is wrong with saying no? Is your guilt legitimate or is it an inbred reaction to the erroneous belief that nice people—especially Christians—don't say no? Think about the value of saying no to everybody concerned. Think what your life would be like if you always said yes.

When I was researching this book, I kept a list of things people asked me to do. Here's what would have happened in one day if I'd said yes to every request. I would have lunched three times that day with three different friends, subscribed to two newspapers, bought a solar heating system, accepted a position as team mother, booked an out-of-town speaking engagement on George's birthday, agreed to have a new carburetor put in my car, and driven to Palm Springs to pick up a prize to be mine if George and I attended a sales meeting about time-sharing vacation property. There's no way I could have said yes to all of that.

The last two questions that allay guilt are these: What are my priorities? and What is God's will for me in this matter? We've already established that we can't take either for granted.

For example, one of my spiritual gifts is teaching. I was a public school teacher for ten years at the elementary level. I worked as a reading specialist and in curriculum development. For a time I taught second grade in the Sunday school at my church. But in His Body, God eventually led me into a teaching ministry with adults, primarily women. So if I am asked, and sometimes I am, to teach children, I say no. That is not because I couldn't do it or am untrained or untalented in that area. It is because that is no longer God's will for me. The most interesting thing about saying yes in such circumstances is that you not only misplace yourself, but you displace the person who should be doing what you're doing. Remember, saying no may be God's will.

RULES FOR SAYING NO THE RIGHT WAY

Saying no is a necessity in time management. The secret is learning how to say it nicely. We can soften the blow by the way we say no. Alan Lakein observed, "This one word,"—NO—"used promptly, properly and with courtesy, can save you a great deal of time. It's important not to let other people fritter away your time, but when you say 'No' you have to make it stick without seeming ruthless or unfair."[6]

Many people put up their guard when they say no because they expect the worst. As a result, they act defensive, instead of firm and sound rude, instead of decisive. The first rule for saying no the right way is to *be polite*. Proverbs 16:23–24 observes, "The heart of the wise teaches his mouth, and adds persuasiveness to his lips. Pleasant words are a honeycomb, sweet to the soul and healing to the bones."

When you say no, watch what you say and how you say it. Use pleasant, persuasive words. Anger, resentment, impatience, and similar feelings may surface while you speak, so note the tone of your voice. Smile and handle the situation with aplomb. Don't make an issue out of saying no, and don't get upset at the other person's reaction to your refusal.

Being polite involves being considerate of other people's feelings. When you decline a request, empathize with the person you're turning down. Thank them for asking you. Offer encouragement: "I know you'll find the right person," or "I'm certain things will work out for you." Offer suggestions, if you have any. Sometimes sharing an idea stimulates a new train of thought and is more constructive than saying yes.

Don't Offer Excuses

A second rule for saying no the right way is *don't offer excuses*. Just say no nicely and give a direct answer. Jesus admonished, "Say just a simple 'Yes, I will' or 'No, I won't'

(Matt. 5:37 LB). A direct no is courteous; evasion is rude, especially when you've already decided your answer will be no. Keeping someone hanging because you don't have the courage to say no wastes their time and causes confusion and frustration. It isn't fair.

Most of us feel we should justify a no answer, so we launch into lengthy explanations. We're not asking for permission to decline, we're saying no. When we explain why we refused, we're inviting criticism. To say, "I can't because . . ." invites someone to automatically reply with several arguments for why our reasoning isn't valid.

My husband is an expert at saying no without making excuses. Through the years, I've watched him decline dozens of requests without getting upset or upsetting anyone. I finally figured out how he does it. He simply says, "I'm going to have to say no to this one." I doubt that he's aware of how forceful, yet polite that statement is. That's saying no the right way: briefly, courteously, and straight to the point.

Develop a Method for Saying No

The third rule for saying no the right way is to *develop a method for saying no*. Robert R. Godfrey noted, "There is virtually no kind of situation that can't be handled with a system." Devising a specific procedure that works for you will help you say no firmly and decisively without getting defensive or irritated. Proverbs 15:28 states, "The heart of the righteous ponders how to answer, but the mouth of the wicked pours out evil things." Having a plan for saying no controls the urge to lash out at others verbally because it forces us to think about how to say no in the least offensive, kindest way and consequently saves a lot of personal aggravation.

One method that Dr. Manuel J. Smith calls "broken record" is extremely effective. If you've ever heard a record that's stuck, you know how this technique works. Basically, it involves saying no repeatedly—over and over and over. Smith says, "You . . . are not deterred by anything the other person may say, but keep saying what you want to say in a *calm, repetitive* voice."[7]

Once you decide you're going to say no, develop a specific "no statement" to use throughout the entire conversation. Dr. Dru Scott suggests that you "practice your new response. Get in touch with how you sound and feel as you say 'NO' in a skillful and thoughtful way. It may not feel 'natural' at first but it will feel natural with practice."[8]

Broken-record no statements work well with everyone, from pesky salesmen to persistent children. I've used this method for so long now that I have a whole repertoire of no statements for specific occasions. For telephone solicitors: "I don't talk to salespersons on the phone unless I call them." For door-to-door salespersons: "I don't buy door-to-door." For anyone who puts me on the spot by asking me to commit to something in front of a group: "I never say yes without consulting my calendar." For kids who push for an immediate answer, trying to force a yes: "We'll discuss it later."

We have to learn to say no if we're going to manage our lives and time. We have to want to do God's will more than we want to please people. We have to do away with the misconceptions and guilt associated with saying no and accept that no is not a dirty word but a useful time-management tool.

We've discussed numerous time-saving devices and covered many life-management concepts in this book. Not all of them will work for everybody. Ultimately, each of us has to pick and choose which ones apply. What matters is that we successfully manage the life the Lord has given us and do whatever is necessary to promote our spiritual and intellectual growth, cultivate a godly character, enhance every relationship, redeem every moment, and glorify God.

It's your life. How you live it is up to you!

WORKSHOP

I. Do you know why you say yes? In column A, list five instances during the past month when you said yes. In column B, list all of the reasons why you said yes.

	Column A	Column B
1.		
2.		
3.		
4.		
5.		

II. Pretend Mr. Smith has just asked you, on behalf of the church board, to serve as chairperson of the building committee. You are qualified. In the space below, describe how you would decide whether or not to accept.

III. Assume you decided to decline the offer to chair the building committee. Now you have to tell Mr. Smith, who

is a very persistent fellow. Develop a no statement to use in
the conversation. Then using the techniques discussed in this
chapter, write how you would respond to each of the
following of Mr. Smith's statements.

1. "I can't tell you how pleased everyone is about your
   being building committee chairperson."

2. "I'm shocked that you're turning this down. The board
   prayed for weeks before asking you. We're sure it's the
   Lord's will."

3. "There's no one in the congregation who is better
   qualified."

4. "We'll get you all of the help you need."

5. "It's not like you to be so stubborn."

6. "The board wouldn't expect you to do another thing at
   the church while you're doing this."

Epilogue

One week after I finished the final draft of this book, the Lord, in His sovereign wisdom, chose to call my beloved George home. Doing the final editing on this manuscript was the most difficult writing assignment I've ever completed. I decided not to delete references to George because he was, and always will be, so much a part of my life and the principles I discuss in this book. I wanted to share with you, my readers, how his death affirmed to me the importance of redeeming our time. None of us has any idea how many days God has allotted us. My heartache would be greatly compounded if I had not invested so much time in my marriage. I have been comforted knowing that I spent quality time with my husband and that not one minute we shared was wasted. I pray that as you read this book, you will keep in mind how truly precious the time we spend with our loved ones is and be motivated to do everything within your power to make every moment count. My hope for you is reflected in David's prayer: "Show me, O Lord, my life's end and the number of my days; Let me know how fleeting is my life" (Psalm 39:4 NIV).

Notes

CHAPTER 1

1. Edward Young (1742–1745), *Night Thoughts,* "Night III."

2. Joan Baez, *Daybreak* (Dial Press).

3. Richard Needham, *The Wit and Wisdom of Richard Needham* (Hurtig, Canada).

4. Sidney Harris, *Field Newspaper Syndicate.* Quoted in *Reader's Digest.*

CHAPTER 2

1. J. I. Packer, *Knowing God* (Downers Grove, Ill.: InterVarsity Press, 1973), 35.

2. Richard Evans, *Richard Evans' Quote Book* (Publishers Press).

3. Warren Wiersbe, *Be Free* (Wheaton, Ill.: Victor Books, 1975), 25.

4. Ibid., 25.

5. Martin Baxbaum, "Points to Ponder," *Reader's Digest* (August, 1984).

6. Gladis and Gordon DePree, *Catch a Red Leaf* (Grand Rapids, Mich: Zondervan, 1980), 1.

CHAPTER 3

1. H. A. Ironside, *Notes on Proverbs* (Loizeaux Bros., 1974), 203, 206.

2. James Allen, *As a Man Thinketh* (Old Tapan, NJ: Fleming H. Revell), 42.

3. Ibid., 12.

CHAPTER 4

1. Edwin Bliss, *Getting Things Done* (New York: Bantam, 1976), 124.
2. Frank B. Minirth and Paul D. Meier, *Happiness Is a Choice* (Grand Rapids, Mich.: Baker, 1978), 55.
3. Ironside, *Notes on Proverbs,* 360.

CHAPTER 5

1. Frank Outlaw, "Points to Ponder," *Reader's Digest* (October, 1981).
2. Curtis Mitchell, *Let's Live* (Old Tapan, NJ: Fleming H. Revell, 1975).
3. Allen, *As a Man Thinketh,* 10.
4. Ibid., 15.
5. Ibid., 29.
6. Wilfred Peterson, "The Art of Reading," *This Week Magazine* (March, 1961).
7. Thomas à Kempis, *Thoughts on the Imitation of Christ* (New York: Golden Press, 1967), 15.
8. W. E. Vine, *Expository Dictionary of Greek Words* (Old Tapan, NJ: Fleming H. Revell), 279.
9. Jessie Penn Lewis, "The Battle for the Mind" (Gospel Literature Crusade).
10. Ibid.
11. Mitchell, *Let's Live,* 82.
12. Thomas à Kempis, *Imitation,* 24.
13. Edward E. Ford, *Why Marriage?* (Niles, Ill.: Argus Communications, 1974), 72.
14 Gerhardt Tersteegen, "The Quiet Way." *Topical Encyclopedia of Living Quotations,* (Minneapolis, Minn.: Bethany House Publishers, 1982).
15. Isabel Moore, "Points to Ponder," *Reader's Digest* (October, 1983).

CHAPTER 6

1. Ronald Kolulak, *Reader's Digest.*

2. S. I. McMillen, *None of These Diseases* (Old Tapan, NJ: Fleming H. Revell, 1958), 110.

3. Wilfred A. Peterson, "Points To Ponder," *Reader's Digest,* (December, 1980).

4. Norman Vincent Peale, *Dynamic Imaging* (Old Tapan, NJ: Fleming H. Revell, 1982), 17.

CHAPTER 7

1. David W. Augsburger, *Caring Enough to Confront* (Ventura, Calif: Regal Books, 1973), 48.

2. Matthew Henry, *Matthew Henry's Commentary* (Grand Rapids, Mich.: Zondervan, 1980), 1872.

3. P. J. Swihart, *How to Live With Your Emotions* (Downers Grove, Ill.: InterVarsity Press, 1976), 57.

4. Ford, *Why Marriage?* 62–63.

5. Norman Wright, *The Christian Use of Emotional Power* (Old Tapan, NJ: Fleming H. Revell, 1979), 17.

6. Vine, *Expository Dictionary,* 147.

CHAPTER 8

1. Vine, *Expository Dictionary,* 152.

2. Elliot D. Abravanel, *Body Type Diet and Lifetime Nutrition Plan* (New York: Bantam, 1983).

3. Ibid., 19.

CHAPTER 9

1. Dennis Hensley, "Points to Ponder," *Reader's Digest* (March, 1983).

2. Hugh Prather, *Notes on Love and Courage* (Doubleday, 1983), Quoted from *Reader's Digest.*

3. Franklin P. Jones, *Quote Magazine.*

CHAPTER 10

1. John W. Alexander, *Managing Our Work* (Downers Grove, Ill: InterVarsity Press, 1972) 6.

2. Bliss, *Getting Things Done,* 67.

3. Dru Scott, *How to Put More Time in Your Life* (1980), 85.

4. Lord Chesterfield, *Letters to His Son* (Rawson, Wade).

5. Alexander, *Managing Our Work,* 13.

6. DePree, *Catch a Red Leaf,* 14.

7. Scott, *How to Put More Time in Your Life,* 66.

CHAPTER 11

1. Vine, *Expository Dictionary,* III, 263.

2. Michael LeBoeuf, *Working Smart* (McGraw Hill, 1979).

3. Russell Tynes, "Points to Ponder," *Reader's Digest* (September, 1981).

4. Don Herold, "Points to Ponder," *Reader's Digest* (May, 1981).

5. Bliss, *Getting Things Done,* 22.

6. Alan Lakein, *How to Get Control of Your Time and Your Life* (Signet Books, 1973), 11.

7. Bliss, *Getting Things Done,* 121.

CHAPTER 12

1. Scott, *How to Put More Time in Your Life,* 187.

2. Ellen Goodman, *Los Angeles Times* (Jan. 20, 1984), part II, 7.

3. Michael Korda, *Success* (New York: Random House, 1977).

4. Bliss, *Getting Things Done,* 100.

CHAPTER 13

1. Lakein, *How to Get Control of Your Time and Your Life,* 84.

2. Manuel J. Smith, *When I Say No, I Feel Guilty* (Dial Press, 1975), 90.

3. Ibid., 91.

4. Ibid., 91.

5. Scott, *How to Put More Time in Your Life,* 36.

6. Lakein, *How to Get Control of Your Time and Your Life,* 85.

7. Smith, *When I Say No, I Feel Guilty,* 63.

8. Scott, *How to Put More Time in Your Life,* 214.